Praise for *Navigating the Impossible*

"Jason is a wonderful storyteller and brings you along on his journeys—what he has learned, how he reflects on that, and what it means for his ability to be successful as a team. A great storyteller who inspires his audiences with his lessons learned. Wow!"
—**Pepijn Rijvers, Senior Vice President of Accommodation, Booking.com**

"I know Jason from my involvement with Muhammad bin Rashid Center for Leadership Development, the center established by His Highness Sheikh Muhammad bin Rashid Al Maktoum, UAE's vice president and prime minister, ruler of Dubai, for the purpose of grooming young leaders to sustain the high speed of growth of the UAE. Jason has unique knowledge and hands-on experience in building record-setting teams. He has learned, through resilience and making it from defeat to being on the top of the podium, what is required to have the most impactful team structure and how to lead such a team to victory."
—**Farhan Al Bastaki, CEO, Sharaf HQ Investment, and author of *Emotional Intelligence in the Life of Muhammad***

"Having worked with Jason for over a decade, I have witnessed his consummate ability to take what he has learned as a world-class performer and teach others how to accomplish goals they believed to be unobtainable. He inspires because he has mastered the brutally tough physical, emotional, and intellectual capabilities required to motivate and effectuate peak performance."
—**John F. Cady, PhD, Professor and Executive Director for Executive Development, Kelley School of Business, Indiana University**

"Jason Caldwell drove and delivered a truly memorable event for my team and me. He was a compelling, insightful, and fully engaging presenter, and I know that the thought-provoking and inspiring experience that he gave us all has certainly influenced our ongoing behavior in a really positive way."
—**Melanie Gallop, President, Calvin Klein/Tommy Hilfiger Europe, Underwear/Swimwear/Sport**

"Jason Caldwell has a God-given prowess to unlock confidence and self-belief in those who need it most. His ability to distill the meaningful from the meaningless, quietly and confidently leading high performance teams to do better, believe more, and ultimately win, is a gift that demands attention."
—**Ian Hogg, former CEO, FremantleMedia Asia Pacific**

"You don't have to be embarking on a world-record-setting adventure to benefit from the incredible teachings of Jason Caldwell. His ability to translate his extraordinary experiences into meaningful everyday leadership and teamwork lessons is unparalleled, leaving audiences inspired and ready to show up as leaders in everyday situations."
—**Anne Rooney, Executive Director, Graduate Programs, Neeley School of Business, Texas Christian University**

"With incredible insight and noteworthy humility, Jason Caldwell distills his daunting experiences into compelling and impactful lessons for leaders in today's complex and volatile world. His stories and the meaningful morals they relate will uplift and equip anyone to better navigate one's own turbulent teams and leadership challenges."
—**Peter Ronayne, PhD, Senior Faculty, Center for Creative Leadership**

"Jason Caldwell's lessons in leadership were exactly what our organization needed to hear. Extremely inspiring and motivating. Our organization has benefitted greatly from the gift of his adventures, and I am very grateful for his contribution. I highly recommend his book."
—**Garry Spence, Senior Vice President, Lincoln Financial Group**

"Capturing experience and distilling it into concrete thoughts and actions is the essential fuel of high performing leaders and teams. Jason has an immense talent that allows him to translate the world he lives in as an adventurer to the issues that face people and organizations. Amazingly, I am as impressed by his intellect and leadership expertise as I am by his physical accomplishments."
—**J. B. Kurish, Senior Associate Dean for Executive Education and Professor in the Practice of Finance, Goizueta Business School, Emory University**

"Damn, that's one hell of a story. You're the f*cking man! Will you sign my arm?"
—**Dennis, drunk guy at a bar in Montana**

NAVIGATING
THE
IMPOSSIBLE

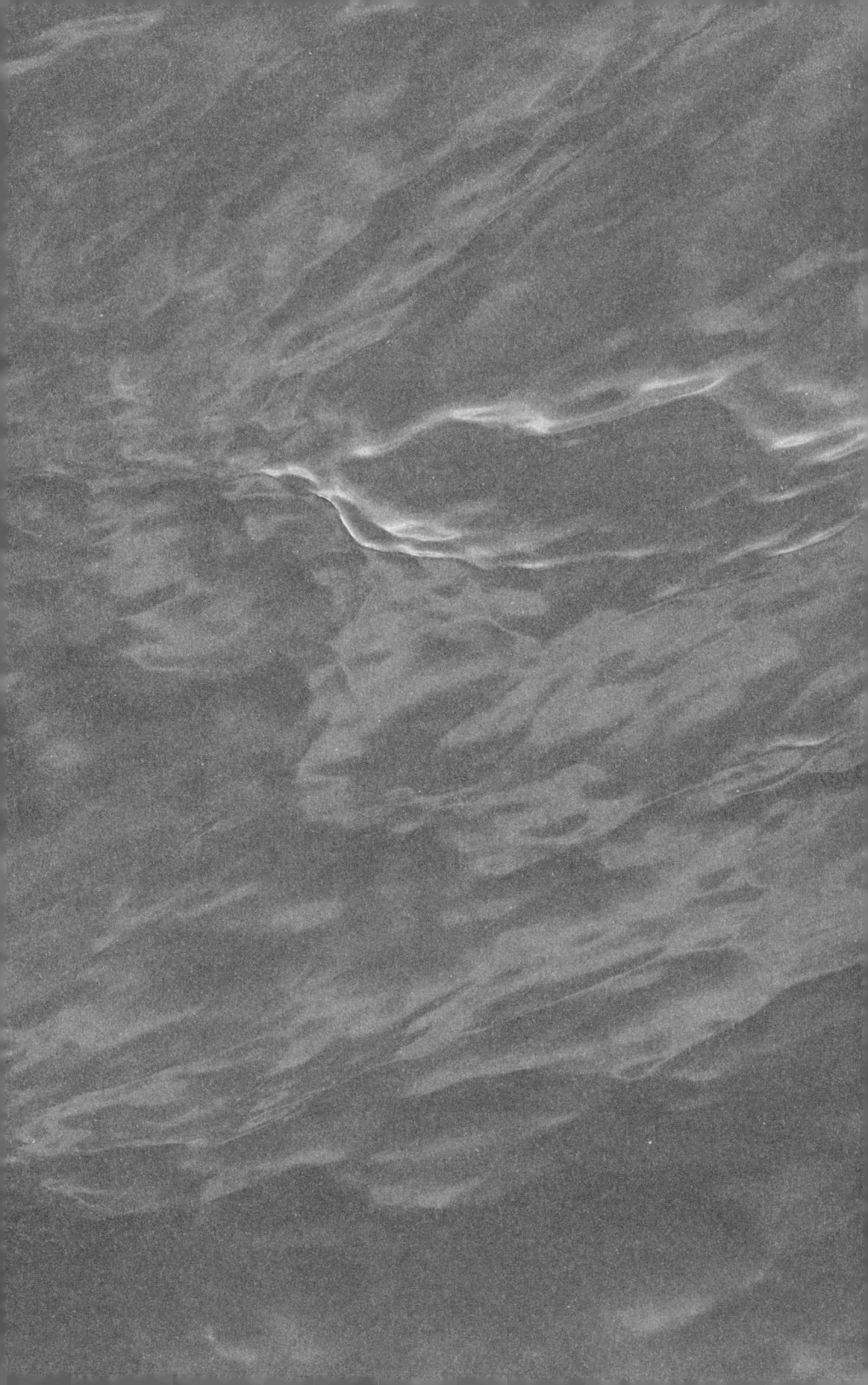

NAVIGATING THE IMPOSSIBLE

BUILD EXTRAORDINARY TEAMS AND SHATTER EXPECTATIONS

JASON CALDWELL

BK·

Berrett–Koehler Publishers, Inc.

Berrett-Koehler Publishers, Inc.
1333 Broadway, Suite 1000
Oakland, CA 94612-1921
Tel: (510) 817-2277
Fax: (510) 817-2278
www.bkconnection.com

ORDERING INFORMATION

QUANTITY SALES. Special discounts are available on quantity purchases by corporations, associations, and others. For details, contact the "Special Sales Department" at the Berrett-Koehler address above.

INDIVIDUAL SALES. Berrett-Koehler publications are available through most bookstores. They can also be ordered directly from Berrett-Koehler:
Tel: (800) 929-2929; Fax: (802) 864-7626; www.bkconnection.com.

ORDERS FOR COLLEGE TEXTBOOK/COURSE ADOPTION USE. Please contact Berrett-Koehler:
Tel: (800) 929-2929; Fax: (802) 864-7626.

Distributed to the U.S. trade and internationally by Penguin Random House Publisher Services.

Berrett-Koehler and the BK logo are registered trademarks of Berrett-Koehler Publishers, Inc.

Printed in the United States

Berrett-Koehler books are printed on long-lasting acid-free paper. When it is available, we choose paper that has been manufactured by environmentally responsible processes. These may include using trees grown in sustainable forests, incorporating recycled paper, minimizing chlorine in bleaching, or recycling the energy produced at the paper mill.

Library of Congress Cataloging-in-Publication Data
  Names: Caldwell, Jason, author.
  Title: Navigating the impossible : build extraordinary teams and shatter expectations / Jason Caldwell.
  Description: First edition. | Oakland, CA : Berrett-Koehler Publishers, [2019] | Includes index.
  Identifiers: LCCN 2019022970 | ISBN 9781523086719 (paperback) | ISBN 9781523086726 (pdf) | ISBN 9781523086733 (epub)
  Subjects: LCSH: Teams in the workplace—Management. | Organizational behavior. | Leadership.
  Classification: LCC HD66 .C345 2019 | DDC 658.4/022—dc23
  LC record available at https://lccn.loc.gov/2019022970

FIRST EDITION

25 24 23 22 21 20 19 || 10 9 8 7 6 5 4 3 2 1

Book producer: BookMatters, Berkeley; Text designer: BookMatters, Berkeley; Cover designer: Wes Youssi, M.80 Design; Copyeditor: Mike Mollett; Proofer: Janet Reed Blake; Indexer: Leonard Rosenbaum

For Amelia
the one who gives meaning to my adventures—
and everything else.

CONTENTS

INTRODUCTION

Far and away the number one question I receive with regard to the adventures and world records I have undertaken is "Why?" Why do you do them? Why do you put yourself through that? What do you get out of these adventures that keeps you going back, pushing boundaries, and testing your limits?

For the first few years of adventuring and training, I didn't have an answer to this question. After some years had gone by and I matured in my ability to process my adventures, I formulated a partial answer. While I couldn't say exactly why I continued to challenge the limits of this world, I had become distinctly aware that whatever it was that I was receiving out there, I was unable to replicate it in my everyday life back home. Not that I have an unhappy home life. I am happily married, with a robust social network and plenty to do. I am never bored and never tired.

It was only recently that I was finally able to answer this one seemingly simple and often repeated question as to why I participate in life the way that I do. Adventure and adversity in this world have taught me, and continue to reiterate to me, one salient lesson that I am desperate to be reminded of: life is too long.

That statement counters the age-old wisdom you were no doubt brought up with—I certainly was. We've been told and are convinced that life is short. Life is too short. But in the world of adventure I've learned that those words have done us a disservice.

Life is not short. It's long, really long. It's so long, in fact, that this idea is what keeps us from achieving the goals we want for ourselves. You put off learning the piano because you just started that new career and you'll get to it once the madness slows down. You wanted to ask out that girl you saw at the coffee shop. But the timing didn't feel right, and you see her in there at least a few times a week; you'll summon the courage next week. You wanted to lose weight, that 10 pounds that's now become 20, but you haven't found that friend who will become your workout partner, and trainers are too expensive. You haven't spoken to your father in years. You can no longer remember what the fight with him was over—maybe it was a series of little things that just became too much. You have a longing to correct it, but you know it will be difficult.

But what have you noticed? Very few people play the piano. That girl has started coming to the coffee shop with someone else. That 20 pounds is looking more like 25. And you've heard your father is in the hospital. You didn't even know he was sick, and you feel the distance for reconciliation is now too great.

What we've all fallen victim to, in one area or another, is giving time too much credit. If you really believed that life is short, you'd be playing the piano by now, you'd be talking to that girl, you'd have patched things up with your dad. But what you really believe is that life is long and that you will always have more time.

That is the reason I push myself to cross endless oceans, trudge through sweltering deserts, and climb mountains of granite. Because life is long, we actually have plenty of time, and I'm afraid that I'll use this as an excuse to live a very ordinary life. I'm afraid that this complacency will take ahold of me like a cancer, and my days will become weeks, my weeks will become seasons, my seasons will become years, and my years will become my life.

Not everyone feels this pressure. Not everyone looks at their life as a mission. But there's a name for people who do. We call them leaders.

This book tells the story of how I built and led one exceptional team and the impossible result we were able to achieve. You will find lessons, and those lessons lead to a process—the process by which I became the type of leader that people were willing to risk not just their careers but their lives to follow.

What I did is interesting, but how I did it is what really matters. I can't teach people how to row or trek or run at my level, but I can teach people how to lead.

There is a difference between teams that succeed and teams that exceed the expectations put upon them. This book is not about building and leading a team that gets the job done. It's about building and leading a team that does what others say cannot be done and then sustaining that high performance over time.

The question I get the most is *why?*, but after reading this book the question you will ask the most is *how?*

How did you lead a team like that? How did you achieve such an incredible result? How did you hang in there when things went from hard to brutal?

How did you do the impossible?

QUIT LIKE A WINNER

I am an adventurer.

This means I make a living by doing things that have never been done before. Whether it's rowing 3,000 miles across the ocean or hiking through a desert that no human has ever crossed, before I do the things I do people call them "impossible." After I'm done, they call them "crazy." I call them "world records."

I love what I do. Those words don't bother me at all. But there are five words that do: "I could never do that."

In addition to being an adventurer, I'm also a teacher. I travel the world teaching business leaders, academics, and others how dangerous those five words can be. I teach them that you don't need to be a six foot five genetic freak like myself to do something amazing. I teach them that even simple goals can, and should, be tackled with the adventurer's spirit. I teach them that they should stop saying, "I could never do that" and start saying, "I could never do that alone."

The real secret to doing impossible things—whether it's something life-threatening or just something career-threatening—isn't learning to be tough, or strong, or magical. It's learning to build, lead, and sustain high-performance teams.

This book is the story of how I built an exceptional team, the process I learned along the way, and how you can use that process to tackle any goal you may be facing. Because no matter how impossible something seems, the right team can make it possible.

This process isn't simple, and it isn't easy, but it is worth it. So let's begin by talking about the darkest day of my life.

AUGUST 2004

Northern California

My left arm is wrapped tight in a sling, but I can still feel it throb every time my heart beats. And it's beating an awful lot.

I have no problem with doctors, but they do seem to make you wait longer when you're panicking. I'm trying my best to stay positive, but every second that ticks by is another jolt in my elbow and another whisper in my ear that the news might be terrible.

Around 400 jolts later, the door finally opens, and my doctor walks in carrying an unnervingly thick chart. He wastes little time before delivering my diagnosis. Suddenly, I wish he'd let me wait a little longer. I can see his mouth moving, but I've stopped listening. He's just confirming what I already feared, what I knew the moment I heard that "pop" on the mound and felt that electric sting spread slowly through my arm, devouring my future as it went.

The medical term for my condition is a tear in the ulnar collateral ligament. Think of a rubber band connecting your elbow to your forearm. Now imagine blasting that rubber band with a cannon ball.

According to the doc, the only fix is a highly invasive reconstructive surgery with a name too complicated to remember. Baseball players have a shorter name for it, a name that strikes fear in the hearts of aspiring professionals around the world:

Tommy John surgery. In that moment, I feel that it might as well be called your-life-is-over-now-Jason surgery.

I leave the office with a prescription for painkillers and an ultimatum: have the surgery, fight through the months of physical therapy, risk permanent injury, and maybe live to throw another day, or... don't.

I've worked my whole life to get to where I am, but I also really want to keep having a life in the future. I don't know exactly what that means, but I am willing to bet it will require at least two functioning arms.

For the rest of the day, I'm a zombie. My feet carry me around the campus of Sonoma State University unseeing, oblivious to my surroundings. I crisscross the property for hours, lost in a world of what-ifs and shit-this-sucks. The only place I don't go is the baseball field.

I've been trying to ignore the weight in my pocket all day, but as the sun begins to set I know I can't stall any longer. I reach in and pull out my cell phone. The number I need to dial is already on the screen. I finally find the guts to hit Send.

My dad answers on the second ring. I've made my decision. I just hope we both can live with what happens next.

AN INTRODUCTION TO HIGH PERFORMANCE

I never went back to baseball. I'm an athlete. I need to be physical in my life. I have to compete against something or someone in order to function. I decided my health was too important to risk on a single sport. You don't hear this a lot from athletes, but quitting is allowed. In fact, it changed my life.

Fourteen years after I walked away from baseball, I walked out of a boat onto a sunny dock in Antigua, an island in the

West Indies. Together with a team of three other men, I had rowed more than 3,000 miles to cross the Atlantic Ocean in 35 days, 14 hours, and 3 minutes. Together, we won the Talisker Whiskey Atlantic Challenge, which I call "The World's Most Impossible Race," shattering a world record that had stood for more than a decade. It did take me two tries, but that's not bad for a guy with a busted elbow.

This is what my team, Latitude 35, does: We race and adventure around the world. Together, we currently hold eight Guinness World Records that span three oceans and four continents. Our job is to do things that haven't been done before. I guess you could say we're in the impossible business. It pays the bills. But the insurance is a nightmare.

Speaking of bills, it turns out that rowing across an ocean isn't just dangerous, difficult, and dangerous (did I say that already?), it's also expensive. Napoleon said that an army marches on its stomach. Well, an adventurer marches, climbs, rows, or runs on his sponsors.

When I set out to get funding for my Atlantic crossings, people told me to call on Under Armour, Red Bull, and all the usual players. I did, but they weren't interested. As it turns out, ocean rowing isn't quite as popular as professional basketball or the X Games.

My sponsor ended up being Carlisle Companies. Carlisle manufactures things that make other things work: wiring harnesses, building materials, machinery—that's all Carlisle. What they do they do well, but they aren't exactly known for their connection to the athletic world. General Mills won't put a high-performance fiber-optic cable on a box of Wheaties no matter how innovative it is. But when I pitched them on my idea, they became the best partner I could have ever asked for.

One of my current sponsors is Booking.com. Its parent company, Booking Holdings, owns most of the online travel solutions you've heard of—Kayak, OpenTable, Priceline, and so forth. The company generated over $12 billion in revenue last year.

Last year, Booking flew me to their corporate headquarters in Amsterdam to speak at their annual meeting. The schedule had me giving my presentation at the same time as people with more business experience and corporate accolades than Gordon Gekko, Don Draper, and Scrooge McDuck combined. I didn't think anyone would choose to hear my boat stories when they could be learning how to shift paradigms and create synergies. I was wrong.

More than 4,000 people crowded Booking's main stage to hear my story. It was standing-room only. I felt like I should be wearing a pinstripe suit and telling them all how "greed is good." For the record, I didn't. Pinstripes don't really work for tall guys.

Joining forces with Carlisle Companies and Booking has reinforced a lesson I've been learning since the early days of my career as a professional adventurer: the corporate world really wants to buy what the competitive world is selling.

Productivity, leadership, efficiency, endurance, discipline, success—these are the traits of elite athletes. They are also the traits that a sales manager in Phoenix or Seattle really wishes he could bottle and slip into his team's morning pot of coffee.

I don't condone spiking company beverages, but I do agree that people who do what I do have learned at least a few lessons that could benefit the world of business. The issue, however, is that we suck at sharing them.

There's a reason that Mount Everest summiteers telling ballrooms full of hungover salespeople to "never give up on their dreams" has become cliché. Empty platitudes and hollow "motivations" seem to abound whenever athletes try to apply their experiences to anyone outside of our little world. If I had a dime for every time I squirmed in my seat as an athlete or adventurer told an audience that the secret to success is simply to put in more effort and never give up, I'd be rich enough to name all my kids Jason regardless of gender. That's called "Foreman money."

I'm a confident guy, but I'm not confident enough to say that I hold the secret to a perfect life. What I do have is experience with extreme success and extreme failure. I've learned from the latter in order to achieve the former. I can tell you from experience that success isn't about refusing to quit. It's about the teams you build and how you chose to lead them.

This book is for people who have a destination in mind and know there are miles to go before they sleep—miles that will be filled with absolutely brutal terrain. It is designed as a guide to teach leaders how to build, sustain, and guide high-performance teams through the challenges they will face in order to capture the glory waiting on the other side. If your only focus right now is collecting a paycheck, then this book is not for you.

But if you're ready to show the world, and yourself, what you're capable of as a leader, stay with me. In the lessons that follow you will learn what I know about creating teams that can, and will, do the impossible. It all starts with a single question: why?

ANSWERING THE QUESTION *WHY?*

I have done incredible things, but I have never achieved anything great on my own. Every record I've set, every stroke I've taken, and every mile I've hiked is made possible by my teams. Not every member of the team may have been with me at the finish line, but they were the ones who ultimately made it possible for me to be able to cross it at all.

Every team I build is meant to do something impossible. Doing the impossible in this case means accomplishing a goal that subverts the expectations of rational people.

Your impossible could be hitting a massive sales quota, starting an innovative new company, or just making sure the people you've hired get to keep their jobs for another quarter. The impossible is all around us, but so is adventure, and adventure can beat the impossible if you do things in the right order. The very first step is answering the question *why?* Not for your team, not for your boss, but for yourself.

Why should you give all your time and effort to this particular goal? If you don't know why you're doing something, if you don't have a crystal-clear image of the success you're chasing and the reason you're chasing it, then you will never lead a high-performance team. You might be able to scrape together a few solid returns out of a burned-out group of overstressed individuals, but it won't last.

If I didn't have a strong why for my team and from my team, we would not have won our world record. We would not have made it across the ocean. We probably would have never even tried.

If all this sounds emotional, that's because it is. Leadership is way more right-brained than people give it credit for. Building strategy is important. Setting timelines is important. Project management is important. But if you don't own the emotions of your team, then you don't really have a team at all.

The only way to reliably build teams that succeed is to find your why and instill it into the hearts and minds of the people you're supposed to be leading. Believe it or not, the first step in finding that why may in fact be quitting.

Quitting is not a failure. Most people have heard that "it's not how many times you get hit that matters; it's how many times you get back up," and that's what they believe.

This saying is inspirational as hell if you're in a *Rocky* movie. But in real life, it's wildly off base. I'm not here to teach you how to be good at getting up. I'm here to teach you how to learn the right lessons from your time on the ground so that when you do get back up, you've become such a strong leader, with such a strong team, that you cannot be knocked down again. And neither can the members of your team.

When we were rowing in the ocean, whenever one of us took a dip in the water we were tied to the boat with a rope in case the currents changed suddenly. The last thing you want is to be untethered in the middle of endless water watching hopelessly as your boat disappears over the horizon.

However, we also always kept a knife on the deck as well. This knife was meant to cut the rope in the event an unexpected wave shifted the boat into a position where it was actually injuring one of our teammates. In life, your why is just like that rope.

Some people are too afraid to bring out their knife. They cling so tightly to an opportunity that they don't realize it's actually strangling them to death. They prefer that choking consistency to the terrifying possibility of being set adrift in an ocean of raw possibility.

Direction is good. Goals are good. But not all goals are created equal, and you need to test and be intentional with your goals to make sure they reflect the unique abilities, emotions, and goals of you and the team you are leading. Then you need to lead the team to the success you promised. In this book you will learn a process through which you can accomplish both of these things.

It starts with finding your why, which may mean calling it quits on a goal that is wrong for your team. But how do you know when the time is right? How do you know if an opportunity is keeping you tethered securely or choking the life out of you?

LEADERSHIP LESSON: UNDERSTAND SUFFERING AND SACRIFICE

Quitting is nothing more than weighing two variables and finding that one of them has stopped being worth it. These two variables are something that every human deals with on a daily basis: suffering and sacrifice.

Humans have a knack for understanding the amount of suffering and sacrifice that they must endure to reach their goals. The trick is that you need to start doing this consciously and channeling what you find into a decision that leads to a why, which leads to a team, which leads to an impossible victory.

As an example, let's look at two different corporate histories.

Airbnb is a company that enables people to open their homes to paying guests. That's a wild idea even today, when as of this writing the company is currently poised for a massive initial public offering (IPO). But it was absolute insanity back in 2008 when its founders, Brian Chesky and Joe Gebbia, started trying to raise millions for a company most people were sure would be used exclusively by serial killers.

The duo persevered, however, and held on to their idea. The hook, they believed, was the ease and intimacy of people

sharing their homes with other people, giving guests the experience of really living in the city they're visiting. That idea
was too powerful to give up, and today the insane company is
projected to receive a post-IPO valuation of $190 billion.

That's one path. But let's consider another.

Very few people have heard of *Game Neverending*, an innovative little internet-only video game from a company called
Ludicorp. The creators of *Game Neverending* dreamed of creating a fully immersive digital world, complete with fluid social
interactions and a real, dynamic economy. The game had trou-
ble getting funding—and players—and soon Ludicorp was on
the verge of collapse.

In the final days of the game's life, one enterprising pro-
grammer launched some simple photo-sharing functionality
into *Game Neverending*'s social system. Photo sharing quickly
became the number one activity among the game's band of
diehard players. This put Stewart Butterfield, Ludicorp's co-
founder and chief executive, in a tough position.

Butterfield could ignore the success of photo-sharing and
leverage the company's remaining funds into a last-ditch effort
to make the game a success—a direction that was championed
by most of his employees. Or he could abandon his dream of
running a gaming company and start building a photo app.

The decision was difficult, but eventually Butterfield decided to scrap the game and launch a photo company instead.
He gave his new start-up an era-appropriate, vowel-discarding
name: Flickr.

Flickr became, in a pre-Facebook world, the number one
photo-sharing website on earth and was eventually acquired
by Yahoo! in 2005 for an estimated $22 to $25 million.

As humans we have an innate desire for comparison. Are

Chesky and Gebbia geniuses for holding on to their idea and building a multibillion-dollar company? Was Butterfield a master strategist for pivoting to photos and earning himself a respectable fortune of his own? The answer to both is the same: not really.

These men aren't special or unique. For every one of them there are thousands more who refused to pivot, or did pivot and ended up with nothing. The lesson here is not that they were successful. It's that they became successful by finding and respecting their own thresholds for suffering and sacrifice.

Every human has an undefined threshold for both suffering and sacrifice that they are unwilling to go past. We don't talk about it. We can't measure it on any objective standard. But it's there, and it's there for everyone.

A noble quitter is someone who understands where that line is and learns to respect it. Quitting has gotten a bad name from people who are unaware of or unwilling to define that threshold and therefore decide to stop before they ever hit it. There is no honor or reason in that sort of quitting.

My adventures have taught me that while we all do have a threshold for suffering and sacrifice, it is usually much higher than we think. A person who would be capable of leading a high-performance team takes the time to learn exactly where their line is. Because once you know it, you can tiptoe right up to the edge and actually go farther than all the other people who flamed out a mile back because they couldn't imagine they could make it that far.

The path to doing difficult things is not mindless enthusiasm. It is to learn about yourself. Learning about yourself is the only way to block out negativity, endure past adversity, and meet the goal you've set. It means testing yourself. It means earning your own self-confidence and paying through hardship. Then you will have the right to say to your team, "This is what we have to do."

Quitting is not failure. Quitting is realizing that this one goal isn't right for you and your team. Failure, real failure, is never finding one that is.

My path to success started the day I quit on something I'd wanted my entire life. That was the first step in a journey that would lead me to discover the process of finding my best goals, forging strong whys, building exceptional teams, and leading them to impossible successes.

SEPTEMBER 2004

Sonoma State University

I'm finally back in the gym. I don't have a sport to train for anymore, but I really don't know how else to spend my time. Sonoma State University is beautiful, but it's not exactly New York.

My elbow has healed a bit on its own. I won't be throwing a curveball anytime soon, but at least I can curl a dumbbell without blacking out. I'm reaching the point in my routine where the world starts to slip away and all I can focus on is the work. I've been depending on this time lately to get me through the long depressing evenings when I know my old team is on the field practicing without me. But just as my thoughts start to scatter, I'm interrupted.

"Jason Caldwell?"

I look up expecting to see someone from one of my classes, but I don't recognize this man at all. He's clearly older than I am, but not by much. He has neatly parted blond hair and a smile that seems just a little too big for his face. "Yeah?" I respond. I had a real knack for conversation back then.

"My name is Mark," he says. "Got a second?"

GATHERING POINT: LEARN HOW TO QUIT

» **Answering the question** *why?* Before attempting any goal, you must answer the question *why?* for yourself. Why should you give all your time and energy and talent to this particular goal or set of goals? You can't start to build and lead great teams without answering this question for yourself.

» **Suffering and sacrifice:** Every commitment you make requires you to weigh two concepts: suffering and sacrifice. To stay committed to a goal means that you are willing to exchange the amount of suffering and sacrifice this goal demands of you. People who say they cannot do something are actually saying they are unwilling to endure the suffering or the sacrifice, or both, that are required of them to complete the task.

» **Productive quitting:** Quitting can be a very productive thing and is often done by those we credit the most with winning. Quitting allows you to focus on a new goal rather than paying the opportunity cost of stubbornly committing to a goal that you don't really find worthy of your time.

LEAD BY EMOTION

Everyone wants to be a part of something greater than themselves.

Every leader on some level knows this, but that knowledge is usually pretty shallow. Most of us lead from strategy first, then analytics, and then maybe emotion if there's time before lunch. But not Mark.

Mark would become my first-ever rowing coach at Sonoma State University in Northern California. He taught me the first and most important lesson of building high-performance teams. That lesson is this: The worst thing in the world is not losing. It's having no purpose.

Mark introduced me to the concept that would go on to become the foundation of my world-record-setting ocean rowing team and every other team I've put together since. It's called "emotion-first leadership," and its results cannot be denied.

But that didn't stop me from trying to deny it.

SEPTEMBER 2004

The Petaluma River

I never thought I would see an inhaler at a tryout. I am experiencing a lot of firsts on this day of tryouts. My first time stepping into a rowing shell. My first time nearly flipping a rowing shell. My first time praying, "Please, God, don't let me die in a rowing shell." How did I let that little blond guy in the gym talk me into this?

There he is, standing in the middle of the room, announcing to his gaggle of sopping-wet rejects that not only had they all done better than he expected, but nobody—that's right nobody—who wants to row for his team will be cut.

What did he just say? This is no longer a sport. This is no longer a competition. This is some kind of day camp for kids who want to splash around between poetry readings. I don't even wait for Mark to finish speaking before I go for the door. I am halfway into my truck when I hear him call my name. This guy seriously doesn't know when to quit.

He starts in on what I am sure will be a just-give-it-a-shot sort of speech. But I want nothing to do with it. I slam the door while he's still talking and peel the heck out of there leaving Mark smiling after me, covered in gravel, mud, and, I hope, a healthy amount of regret.

I want to get as far away from Mark as I can and never look back. If it hadn't been for Mike, I probably would have.

MIKE

"Hey, are you Jason?"

Seriously, what is it with people talking to me during a workout? I almost drop the weight I am lifting but manage to get it back into the rack without breaking my neck. I turn around angrily but am surprised to see someone I actually recognize. He's been in here almost as much as I have lately.

Mike is shorter than I am, with dark hair, sharp features, and bright, friendly eyes. He's the kind of guy who can come up to a total stranger at the gym, startle them into almost killing themselves, and not get punched, which is a really good skill for him to have at that moment. I shake his hand instead of throttling him, and we start to chat. It turns out, we have a lot in common.

Mike used to be a soccer player until one bad fall took him out of the game for good. Just like me, Mike wasn't ready to call it quits. Just like me, Mark got him to the rowing tryout. Just like me, Mike thought the whole thing was a joke. Unlike me, Mike wasn't an asshole about it.

We agree that Sonoma State's "team" leaves a lot to be desired, but Mike is determined to give rowing a shot. He asks me to consider doing the same. Maybe we'll be able to push each other and keep some last ember of our competitive fires burning.

"Besides," he says, "I could really use a ride to the boathouse."

To this day, I'm grateful Mike couldn't afford a car.

ROWING 101

US collegiate rowing is like a solar system. At the center is the Ivy League. Harvard, Yale, Princeton, Penn—these schools have access to the best recruits, the best equipment, and the best natural rivers in the country. These programs are considered incubators for Olympic athletes. They win. A lot.

Orbiting around the Ivies are the standouts—schools that have intentionally invested the time, money, and energy it takes to compete with the best student crew teams in the nation. Mercury is Stanford; Mars is Washington; Jupiter is Cal; Venus is Ohio State. You get it.

In terms of this aquatic starscape, Sonoma State wasn't exactly in the same orbit. Or galaxy. Or universe. It existed in some parallel reality where boats seemed to weigh twice as much and trophy cases were supposed to be empty. At that time, Sonoma State had never won a single race. Ever.

But Mike and I kept our word. We beat the sun getting up every morning and never missed a single one of Mark's training sessions. True to his word, Mark never cut anyone. He left that up to the river.

We rowed in eight-oared sweep boats. That means eight guys the size of pine trees have to fit themselves into a single shell without flipping it over or sinking it or both.

Sweep rowing means that each man has one oar instead of two. It also means that a crew has to take every stroke in perfect unison. One out-of-sync blade in the river can take crucial seconds off your time. Or send you careening into something much more solid than water. Or both.

The skill, physicality, and patience this sport requires— combined with a 5:00 a.m. call time for practice—meant that most of the asthmatic poets I saw at tryouts were long gone. What remained was a real, honest-to-goodness crew. A crew with one odd thing in common.

As Mike and I got to know our new teammates, we realized that almost all of them were like us. Most of them were elite performers in other sports before an injury, being cut from a team, or burnout sent them careening out of competition.

And straight into Mark.

FEBRUARY 2004

Sonoma State Boathouse

We are washing our hand-me-down shells after practice one day when a gleaming silver van comes roaring gracefully up to our boathouse. The van is massive, but it starts to look like a clown car once the doors open and the largest men I've ever seen start pouring out.

From the back of the van, these titans unload sleek,

beautiful shells that make ours look like hollowed-out logs with sloppy coats of silver paint. This is the kind of gear Mike and I have taken to researching longingly after practice every day. Each shell is perfectly polished and unblemished with the exception of a single, large crimson *S*. Stanford.

In terms of ranking and recognition, Stanford's team is so far above ours we need a telescope just to see the bottom of their shoes. What the hell are they doing at Sonoma State?

As it turns out, Mark has invited them. And as it turns out, they are there to annihilate us.

Per Mark's request, Stanford started dropping by and practice-racing us every few weekends. We'd struggle just to keep our stern in line with their bow for a few quick 1,000-meter sprints. Then they'd pack up their shiny toys and go home. Lather, rinse, repeat. Sob.

Mark would follow along in his motorized launch, smiling and chatting calmly with the Stanford coach. He never seemed embarrassed by his team's performance. He never railed at us for getting trounced in every race. But he didn't have to. We were already pissed.

Guys started staying late after each dose of biweekly humiliation to talk strategy. Emails started flying about ways to shave an extra few seconds off our time. Mike and I scheduled extra workouts for the team. A core group of diehard Sonoma State rowers were starting to come together. We had one goal: make Stanford eat shit.

Slowly but surely we crept up on our rivals. We finished 100 meters behind them, then 50 meters, then 12. Soon our bow was close enough to kiss that big red *S*. They weren't exactly eating shit. But, for the first time ever, neither were we.

Their coach noticed. All that effort earned winless Sonoma State an invitation to the Stanford Invitational. Northern California's best rowing programs would all be there. Most of them would be competing in multiple races, but we were given only one.

No pressure, right?

APRIL 2004

Redwood Shores Rowing Course

The oar feels good in my calloused hands. My back strains as I push the blade down into the water. My legs growl with electric heat as I push and pull with all my might. The shell soars across the surface of the water as I push and pull and push again.

I want to turn, just for a second, and check on the other shell. I know it has to be close enough to reach out and touch by now. But I don't. I can't break the rhythm. We have to win this.

Sacramento State isn't exactly Stanford. But they aren't exactly us either. They've won actual races against actual opponents. Today, those opponents are us.

We're 1,200 meters from the finish line. Now 750 meters. Now 500 meters.

I don't turn my head. I keep my eyes fixed on Mike's back, following his rhythm, matching his breath. All I can hear is the whoosh of oars slicing into the water and the roars of both boats' coxswains barking orders to their crews.

The burn in my legs crescendos to a panicked scream. The oar starts to feel slick as sweat pours off me in buckets. 400 meters...300 meters...200 meters. At 50 meters a silent charge runs through the boat. I don't have to turn and look to see the other team. I know where they are—behind us. Sonoma State isn't winless anymore.

Somehow, this team of broken, rejected, burned-out athletes has done something that previously seemed impossible. Together, we have achieved an impossible goal.

And there at the finish line, smiling as always, is Mark.

LEADERSHIP LESSON:
LEVERAGE HUMAN EMOTION

That was our first win, but it wasn't our last. We didn't go undefeated by any means, but we took down plenty of schools that a year before would have demolished our program. The wins felt good. Being back on a team felt even better.

So how did we do it? How did a winless coach with a motley crew become our school's first-ever winning rowing team? The secret was Mark and his ability to do what so few leaders can do these days: create a team that's built on emotion.

If you met me, you might not pinpoint me as an emotional person, but I am. No, I don't cry at sunsets or write poetry about butterflies, but that's not what I mean when I talk about an emotional man or an emotional leader. Being emotional for me means that I have the ability to understand and leverage the emotions of other people—especially the people on my teams.

Leveraging human emotion is the most powerful thing a leader can do if you want to create a high-performance team. To do that you need to understand that humans, at their core, are far more emotional than they are practical. Therefore, your time is better spent engaging the emotions of your team than appealing to their sense of strategy or their professional intuition.

This ability is what makes the difference between a team that can hit a goal and a team that can pull off the impossible. If all you can leverage is your team's minds, time, or bank accounts, their objectives at that level will always be out of your reach.

Mark did this better than anyone I had ever met. By talking to other teammates, I eventually figured out how he did it. We may have seemed like a band of misfits, but Mark didn't just happen upon any of us. He went looking for us.

He went to every other coach on Sonoma State's campus and asked them for a list of names—the names of every single athlete who had been cut, had burned out, or had been injured on their way off a collegiate team. That was his recruiting list. He wasn't looking for blue-chip recruits. He was looking for rejects, castoffs, and burnouts. Once he found us, he went to work.

Mark knew that something awful had happened to every single athlete on his list. I'm not talking about the pain of an injury or the embarrassment of a cut. I'm talking about the soul-rending agony of our greater aspirations being ripped from us. As athletes we'd spent our whole lives pursuing victory. The whole it's-just-about-having-fun thing never holds true for elite performers. At least not for the ones who win.

But Mark never, ever, promised us that we'd win regattas. In fact, he barely talked about winning. He even went so far as to ask us if we even wanted to compete before every major race. That's insane.

Leaders don't ask their teams if they want to do something. They tell them. But Mark asked us if we wanted to compete not because he was shy or weak. He asked us because he knew he didn't have to tell us. He didn't need to demand our best effort.

Our emotions were already leveraged, and we were demanding that effort of ourselves.

But we ate it up. Even big, strong, proud Jason, competing in a sport he had considered a waste of time just weeks ago, quickly found himself pulling harder and training longer than anyone else. Why? Because by recruiting and training us misfits, Mark gave us the only thing that any good leader needs to offer a high-performance team: purpose.

UNLOCKING HIGH PERFORMANCE THROUGH EMOTION-FIRST LEADERSHIP

Rowing is the ultimate team sport, so Mark knew he didn't need a deep bench; he just needed a small, emotionally leveraged team to win. He didn't need people who were just tall. He needed people who cared.

There are two ways to look at any team. You can either try to fire, transfer, and hire your way to a team that, on paper, looks great. Or you can be leader. High-performance teams aren't built; they are forged. And if you're doing your job as a leader, any human soul can be properly forged in your furnace.

Consider this example: Say you're a team leader on an important project. You have a member of your team who is underperforming and threatening the project's success. This is where you make your first choice. You can judge this teammate on his numbers and fire him, or you can think of him as an emotionally driven human being and talk to him. You decide to talk to him.

When you talk to him, you ask why he's struggling. This is important: high-performance leaders always ask questions first. Remember, your job is not to force success; it's to find that something greater that will leverage your team into pursuing success whether you ask them to or not.

When you talk to your teammate, you discover that he just found out his wife is pregnant and he's terrified about the prospect of providing for a growing family. Here you make your second choice.

A standard leader might listen, nod, empathize, and encourage the teammate to keep his head up because losing his job or missing a bonus will only make things harder. The leader might even offer to stay late and help with the teammate's work. But kindness as a leader is not enough to give this person leverage. Being nice is not enough to unlock high performance.

Instead, you look him in the eye and make him a promise. You tell him you're going to make him a plan. This plan will include performance milestones, intense goals, and regular performance reviews. If he hits those goals, you promise him you will do everything in your power to guarantee him a healthy raise and plenty of paternity leave to take care of his new child.

That teammate is going to leave the office ready to run through a wall for you. Now, instead of just feeling heard, he feels empowered. You haven't solved his problem for him. You've offered him a path to the life he wants for himself and the people he cares about.

Books upon books are written about motivation, but it all really boils down to this: you sit your team down, you ask them what they want to be, and then you create for them the opportunity to be what they want. That's what leveraging emotion is all about. Give people not money, time off, or a kind shoulder to lean on. Give them purpose.

Your job as a leader is not to manage anyone. It's to discover, champion, and maintain the something greater that keeps all members of the team leveraged and managing themselves. That's why none of us quit the team. That's why the weekly thrashings by Stanford only made us work harder. And that's why we became the first winning rowing club in Sonoma State history. We did it together.

High-performance teams are made up exclusively of emotionally leveraged people who are determined to achieve the something greater offered to them by a high-performance leader. Nobody gets up at 5 a.m. and rows 10,000 meters because they like their coach. They do it because at the end of those meters is the person they truly want to become.

MAY 2005
Sonoma State University

Mark is an unassuming guy, and his office is just as unassuming as he is. He looks at me thoughtfully over a computer that's older than he is as I wait anxiously to hear what he has to say.

Mark and I have come a long way together. Our team's win against Sacramento has led to many more wins. The man sitting in front of me has given me a new passion, a new skill, a new challenge, a new life. He's about to do it again.

It's time for me to leave Sonoma State. For the record, I've graduated. My degree (in finance) will really come in handy out on the Atlantic. But the postcollegiate career of a rower isn't exactly clear. It's not like there's a draft for us. We're lucky if the World Championships get on ESPN2 at midnight during an NBA lockout.

"You've got an offer," Mark finally says, and I sit up as straight as I can on my chair.

His smile is as big as ever as he tells me where I'm headed. But, for the first time ever, mine might be just a little bit bigger.

GATHERING POINT:
EMOTION IS EVERYTHING

» **Be an emotion-first leader:** Leaders are comfortable with being emotional, and leaders of high-performance teams take that to an even higher level by leveraging the human emotion of the people they are leading.

» **Offer something greater:** The first step in leveraging human emotion is to create something bigger than yourself— something that your team genuinely wants to be part of.

» **Try:** Sustaining this emotional leverage means building and sustaining trust. Your team must believe that you have their best interests at heart. This does not mean getting them everything they want. It means that you care enough to listen and to try to get them to where they want to be.

WIN BEFORE YOU RACE

Chariots of Fire is a great movie about great runners. It mostly follows the athletic career of Olympic sprinter Eric Liddell. Liddell famously won the gold in the 400 meters at the 1924 summer games in Paris after refusing to run his best event, the 100-meter dash, for religious reasons.

Before the Olympics, Liddell ran at the University of Edinburgh against his nemesis: Cambridge sprinter Harold Abrahams. Abrahams would have been the fastest man in Europe if it weren't for Liddell, and he knew it.

After losing one particularly heartbreaking heat to Liddell, Abrahams laments to his girlfriend, Sybil Gordon, that if he can't win he won't run. Gordon logically responds that if he doesn't run he can't win.

I'd like to take that statement a step further. I'd like to say that races aren't where high-performance teams win at all. They're just where they go to pick up the medals.

JUNE 2005

Boathouse Row

Pre-elite. That word really bothers me. You often hear the term in athletic circles, but in reality it's meaningless. How can something be *pre*-elite? That's like being pre-hungry or pre-tired or pre-dead.

Anyone with a pulse and a few firing neurons could be considered pre-elite at one thing or another. I wasn't the best student in school, but maybe I was just a pre-elite Rhodes scholar. This is an honorific that grants zero significance to its subject. It's a meaningless title. But the day I arrived at number 10 Kelly Drive all I wanted was to have the term apply to me.

ROWING ON MOUNT OLYMPUS

America has so many incredible natural wonders. The redwoods, Yellowstone, Yosemite, the Grand Canyon. Their beauty is life changing. But for my money this country's best feature isn't in the deserts of Arizona or the mountains of California. It's in Philly.

The Schuylkill River runs northwest to southeast for 135 miles and goes straight through eastern Philadelphia. Back in the day, it sent enough coal out and brought enough money in to make Philly the most populous and powerful city in America. Today, the coal doesn't flow like it used to, but the river has managed to find a new primary export. Rowers. Damn good ones.

The Schuylkill has played host to more notable rowing competitions than almost any other waterway in the world. But that isn't because the river is perfect. In fact, the Schuylkill does something that no competitive rowing surface should ever do. It bends.

That's right: there's a big, fat, annoying turn about 1,000 meters into the raceable portion of the Schuylkill. Rowing is all about timing, technique, consistency, and synchronization. Even a subtle curve can clip valuable seconds off a boat's time, and the Schuylkill's big left hook is less subtle than Gilbert Gottfried stepping on a Lego.

FISA, the international governing body that sets the rules for competitive rowing, has officially banned rivers with turns. But the Schuylkill has been hosting races since before FISA even existed. It's so old as a racing venue and so respected that it doesn't have to play by the rules. Basically, it's the Clint Eastwood of rivers.

As a result, the factories and refineries that once dotted its wide banks have now been replaced by dozens and dozens of rowing clubs. These clubs range from happy homes for weekend warriors to full-time lodgings for the most successful rowers on the planet. The thing the Schuylkill draws in large numbers is past, present, and future Olympians.

These champions, and their clubs, are grouped into a tightly packed collection of Victorian architecture on the river's east bank. Most people would walk right past this clump of vintage domiciles on their way to the art museum or the boardwalk without a second thought. But for rowers this is hallowed ground, sacred space. It is Kelly Drive, or, as it is more commonly known, Boathouse Row.

Number 12 Boathouse Row is Penn AC, a breeding ground for gold medalists dating all the way back to 1871. Number 11 is College Boat Club, the official boathouse for the University of Pennsylvania's Ivy League rowing program. Number 14 is the Philadelphia Girls' Rowing Club, the first all-female rowing club. Number 12 is Malta Boat Club, and connected directly to it is number 10. Vesper.

When rowers graduate from college programs, their future is far from guaranteed. Most rowers put the communications or advertising degree they earned while competing to use and join the white-collar workforce. Others start coaching the next generation of hopefuls. A small number get placed on some form of semiprofessional rowing team in the hopes of improving their game and moving up the chain. An even smaller number—only a few hundred athletes at most—are taken in by one of the few professional, nationally competitive programs in the country. These programs are called "the elites."

Among the elite programs, the clubs on Boathouse Row are the most competitive and have the best track record when it comes to turning out world record holders and Olympic medalists. Vesper is in the top two or three clubs on Boathouse Row in any given year.

Getting into Vesper is like getting into Harvard or Yale. Staying at Vesper is like getting into Harvard or Yale while also running for president. Getting placed on one of Vesper's top-tier national teams is like getting into Harvard or Yale while running for president as you win the lottery.

It's not an easy thing to do. Most people who live, train, and compete on Boathouse Row come from Ivy League schools, perennial powers like the University of Washington, or top-of-the-line foreign programs like Oxford or Cambridge. They definitely do not come from a bottom-tier team whose biggest claim to fame is "we didn't lose as much as people thought we would."

So it was hard for me not to vomit as I reached out to knock on Vesper's door for the very first time.

THE WORST OF THE BEST

Before I left for Vesper, Mark took me aside. "Look," he said. "It's incredible that Michiel accepted you, but you need to understand. I haven't prepared you for this. What they do and how they do it is way beyond what you're used to. You honestly aren't ready for what's coming."

As far as pep talks go, this one kind of stank. But I managed to do what all 22-year-olds do best: ignore advice, lie to myself, and charge headlong into disaster.

On day one, at my very first Vesper training session, I was told we'd be indoors working on the ergs (short for ergometers, indoor rowing machines). Perfect! I had the best erg times at Sonoma State by far. This was my chance to show these Ivy League trust fund kids how we do things on the West Coast.

Have you ever been so wrong that looking back you wonder why your future self didn't show up in a time machine to slap you in the face and scream, "What the hell is wrong with you?" I was about to have a moment like that.

Either on the erg or in a shell, the longest I'd ever had to row was seven minutes. Seven minutes was my maximum. Which is why my heart dropped down to my toes when I heard Coach announce that day's routine. That day we were each expected to row four 20-minute pieces on the erg with four minutes of rest in between. That's 80 minutes of effort, and I'm not talking about that just-do-your-best kind of effort. I'm talking about that crush-this-or-we'll-see-you-back-in-California-Jason kind of effort.

I knew I was going to be suffering. If I wanted to stay at Vesper—if I wanted to keep moving toward my goal—I would have to go more than 10 times longer than my current limit. This was going to hurt. A lot. But, like most of the suffering we face in pursuit of our dreams, it was optional.

I would be lying if I said I didn't think about quitting right there on the spot. "Why not?" a voice inside me asked. "What's the point of destroying your body for the next 80 minutes when you're already the worst person on the team? Maybe this is a sign. Maybe you just aren't cut out for this. Maybe you should have gotten that surgery after all." But as bad as this was going to hurt, I knew I could take it. I knew it would not surpass my threshold for suffering, and I was ready to make the sacrifice.

Pain is an amazing teacher. Even being near it can show you who you are and what you care about. In that moment, I knew that going forward would mean more pain than I had ever felt in my entire life. But I also knew that, despite the discomfort, I still wanted what was beyond it. Once again, agony was guiding me to the life I wanted most.

The kindest thing I can say about myself that first Vesper practice is that I survived it. My times were high but wouldn't get me kicked out immediately, and low enough to raise Coach's eyebrows as he passed my station.

SEAT RACING

If you start rowing competitively in the United States, you'll typically begin your training in a two-, four-, or eight-person boat. This method teaches hopefuls how to row with a team first and then slowly identifies the standout athletes through a process called "seat racing."

Seat racing works on the principle that it's really hard to figure out how good an individual rower is inside a team boat. In a sport that's all about teamwork and group precision, singling out one rower's skill takes time. Here's how it works.

Coach wants to know how good Racer A is as opposed to Racer B, so he puts together teams in two boats. Each boat contains one of the racers and seven of her elite teammates. Coach then has these two boats race and measures their times. Then he has Racer A and Racer B switch places and has the boats race again. By running this drill a few times and measuring each boat's performance, Coach can make a realistic determination that one rower is more successful than the other when placed in identical conditions. While it's not a perfect system, it usually works, and it's used by just about every notable rowing program in the world. That was a problem for me.

Back at Sonoma State I was the biggest, strongest guy on the team. But while I was there, I struggled to win seat races against guys I would crush in an individual race or erg time trial. I was supposedly a leader on that team, but my losing streak got so bad that Mark eventually had to start putting me in the top boat based on his own instincts rather than my performance on the water. I performed well, but I was also becoming an Adam Sandler—someone who manages to earn his higher-ups a fortune even though he also made *Jack and Jill*.

The specter of my seat racing struggles came with me to Philly and Vesper's style of boat selection. All things being equal, an American rower could go their entire career without ever rowing a shell by themselves. This makes it easier to be selected for seat races and work your way up to the top boats. I was an American athlete, but my coach was Michiel Bartman—who may be the most European man who has ever lived.

It's hard enough to qualify for the Olympics once; Michiel did it three times. He rowed for the Netherlands in Atlanta (1996), Sydney (2000), and Athens (2004), where he won gold, silver, and silver, respectively. He's built like Dolph Lundgren's slightly smaller brother, and he's fluent in the ancient Dutch language of "saying exactly what you think to anyone, anytime, anywhere, no matter how they might feel about it." Michiel is not the guy to ask if you look fat in that new outfit—unless you want to hear exactly how fat you look and how perhaps it's time for a haircut as well.

During his days as a competitive rower, Michiel was known as one of the most brilliant rowing tacticians in the world. He had the uncanny ability to perfectly time his practice rows in order to make sure he nailed it on race day. That strategic genius propelled him to three Olympic medals and several world championships.

This is a man who has succeeded at the highest levels of his craft. And he would be my coach for every stroke I pulled at Vesper. He would routinely annihilate my confidence in one breath and then give me a perfect strategy for improvement in the next. I have never been more terrified of, or more grateful to, any person in my entire life.

European rowers start their training in a single shell. Before they can even get into a seat race, they have to prove they know how to handle the mechanics and compete on their own. European clubs believe that the key to building strong teams is to first build strong individuals.

Today, I wholeheartedly agree. In fact, it's become one of my core philosophies. Back then, however, I was miserable. Until I started posting better times in a single, I couldn't even buff a team boat after practice. This meant I couldn't even be selected for a seat race and THAT meant my chances of making the year-round team looked slim as I struggled along in my lonely solo shell. But, suddenly, there was hope.

The USRowing National Championships were taking place in Indianapolis that year. I had no business being invited, but even a scrub on Vesper is still on Vesper. To my utter disbelief, Michiel informed me I would have the chance to compete in the biggest race of the year. I would be entered as a single, but so what? As long as I didn't finish in last place, everything would be fine.

AUGUST 2005

USRowing National Championships, Indianapolis

I finish in last place.

As the final shell screams across the finish line, the people around me are whooping and cheering while I pray very hard for the ground to open up and swallow me. Dead last. I have never been dead last at anything, ever in my life. But numbers don't lie; it is now official.

I need to get some help.

A LESSON FROM DON WIPER

Everyone loves Don Wiper. Don was a mainstay at Vesper when I first arrived, and he remains a good friend to this day. But back then I wasn't looking for a friend; I was looking for a teacher. And Don was known for one thing at Vesper: he never, ever, lost a seat race.

Don was getting on his bike when I caught up to him after practice. "Hey, Don!" I shouted as he strapped on a helmet that clearly wasn't designed for someone his size.

He looked up and smiled as he saw me coming. Don is always smiling. "What's up, Jay?" he asked. Only a handful of people on the planet get to call me Jay. Don is one of them.

Oh crap! Good question. What exactly was up? Even though Don and I got along great, I was suddenly terrified. How do you ask someone you respect—someone who's clearly better than you are at something you're both trying to excel at—how to improve? Take it from one very nervous 22-year-old; the direct approach is best. "I wanted to ask you how you always win your seat races," I sputtered.

Struggling in a single, I wasn't even in a position to be chosen for a seat race yet, but Don didn't seem surprised by my question at all. If anything his smile got bigger. "It's actually not as complicated as you might think," he replied. "Think about it like this. Seat racing isn't just about you, right? There are seven other guys in that boat with you. You know how we all say we pull hard for everyone no matter what?"

This was true. In rowing it's a MAJOR unwritten rule that you do your absolute best for the guy or gal being seat raced no matter who they are. Because next time it could be you.

"Well, we both know that isn't always how it goes," Don continued. "There's something inside of people that unlocks for things they care about and shuts down for things they don't. If you hate a guy, you can be as honorable as they come, but there will always be 1 percent of you that isn't doing its best. But if you care about him, I mean *really* care about him, you'll go well past 100 percent to get him where he wants to go."

I like to think I was nodding wisely as Don talked that day, but in reality I was probably drooling with my mouth open. This was it. This was the key to everything. Suddenly, the doors were open, and I was staring at the secret to achieving high-performance, emotion-first leadership.

You win races by winning people.

LEADERSHIP LESSON:
BUILD AUTHENTIC TRUST

One of Michiel's favorite sayings is that "the winter is where you win your medals; the summer is just where you go to pick them up." I always took that to mean that it's important to train hard in the winter off-season so you're ready to win the summer regattas. But Don's philosophy on seat racing showed me that it's not about strengthening yourself physically. It's about strengthening your team emotionally.

Here's the important thing to remember: a team becomes high performance well before the test that actually defines it. The mistake is to put the cart before the horse and try to classify you or your team as high performance by throwing it up against an impossible challenge. This common misconception can easily burn teams out and leave leaders chasing their tails.

High-performance teams aren't high performance because they do something hard; they do something hard because they're high performance. High-performance teams are different from other teams in one major way: they are completely dependent on one another. It's all about emotion. The vital interdependence of high-performance teams is created by leveraging a single emotion: trust. So when we talk about performance, we first need to talk about trust.

Trust with regard to high-performance teams is not the act of doing what you say you're going to do. It's the act of *trying* to do what you say you're going to do. It's not about results or strategic brilliance. It's about authenticity.

As the leader of a team, you leverage trust with your teammates through genuine, authentic effort. This effort was displayed beautifully by Don, who was always trying to make the athletes around him better.

Don would go to extra practices, double up on exercises, and always be the guy who kept the rest of us from making asses of ourselves at the bar. It's important to note that those aren't all decisions about "work." But they are all high-performance decisions that authentic leaders use to build and leverage trust.

Vesper is a team of battle-hardened elite performers. They don't display their emotions easily. The team didn't trust Don because he was the best rower; he wasn't. They trusted him because he convinced them that he genuinely had their best interests at heart. If you're a leader, that is your job, too.

Here's the good news: You don't have to be the best in the world at what you do to earn trust, which was great news for me during my first abysmal summer at Vesper. You just have to be authentic and consistent.

Don was not the best rower on our team. He wasn't the most skilled or the fastest. But the rest of the crew knew with 100 percent certainty that he was going to give them everything he had. His authenticity created trust, that trust created a bond, and that bond leveraged our entire team to the point that they had no choice but to pull past their limits. Don wasn't the best at rowing. But he was the best at building trust, and that trust made him the best.

Here's the bad news: I can't tell you how to be authentic. There's no checklist or rubric to follow. You can't fake it, and if you try, you could ruin the very trust you're trying to create. Don't read this and think all you have to do is ask the guy at work about his baby and he'll bend over backward to help you meet your deadline.

Stay with me here: the type of authenticity that builds elite-level trust is similar to pornography. In his landmark ruling, Supreme Court Justice Potter Stewart said of pornography, "There is no one definition of what it is. But you know it when you see it." And so does your team.

A high-performance team needs to trust more than just its

leader. The individual team members must also trust one another implicitly. The leader's job is to prioritize and foster this trust—to turn the people he leads away from the individual ego of self-interest to the collective ego of team interest. This cannot be faked.

The best way to be authentic and build this type of trust on your team is to worry less about the alignment of your strategies and more about the alignment of your own emotions. Do you *care* about your people? Are you more concerned about who they are becoming, or do you care only about what they are capable of producing for your bottom line? Do you pull hard for them before asking them to pull hard for you?

If your answer to those questions is yes, then you don't need a checklist to build authentic trust. Emotion-first leadership goes both ways. In order to leverage your people, you also need to make sure you're letting them leverage you.

JUNE 2011

Back on Boathouse Row

After my discussion with Don, I made a difficult choice. I decided to leave Vesper and return to Sonoma State for an extra year. I had some unfinished business to attend to.

That year at Sonoma, armed with my first few lessons in emotion-first, high-performance leadership, I never lost a single seat race, and together we rowed the most successful crew season in the school's history.

Michiel follows our success and invites me to return to Vesper for another shot at the year-round team. Once again, Don's lessons pay off. I not only make the team; I make the top boat as well. Three years after being the worst rower on the best team, I finally earn my place as a member of a true rowing elite. Not just because I have become stronger but because I have become a guy who the other guys genuinely want in that boat along with them.

There is then only one challenge left to conquer: the Olympics.

GATHERING POINT:
THE COLLECTIVE EGO

» **Results come second:** High-performance teams are defined not by the results they achieve. They are defined by how they interact with one another and the outside influences acting upon them. The amazing results are simply a by-product of these high-performance relationships.

» **Complete interdependence:** High-performance teams are unique in that there is complete interdependence among the teammates. They become a delicate and complex organism that breaks down if you take out the most seemingly insignificant player.

» **You have to care:** Leaders aren't the only ones whom the team needs to trust. They must also trust one another implicitly. Authentic trust comes from being more concerned about the collective ego of the team than about your individual ego. This cannot be faked.

GATHERING POINTS

Connecting your team to its something greater is everything for a high-performance leader. At Vesper, you don't have to ask any of the men or women on the team what that something greater is for them. It is literally hanging in our trophy case: Olympic gold medals.

Boats rowed by Vesper athletes took home the gold in the 1900 London Olympics, the 1904 St. Louis Olympics, and the 1964 Tokyo Olympics. To this day, Vesper is the only rowing club in the world to field three gold-medal-winning teams in the eight-man race.

The achievements of the past aren't what fuel the athletes of the present, however. Michiel employed similar emotion-first leadership tactics that had worked so well for Mark back at Sonoma State. He knew that winning a shiny trophy wasn't a strong enough why to drive an athlete to the level of an Olympic performer. But winning that trophy for the other guys in your boat damn sure was.

Thanks to the advice of Don Wiper, my return to Sonoma State, and my subsequent return to Vesper, I was finally in a place to push for the goal I had been leveraged for years to desire. I owe my success not to my own abilities but to my ability to operate as a member of a high-performance team.

I was no longer a college student, and neither were my teammates. I and the men rowing with me at this point in my career were fully formed, elite athletes. It would be a few more years until I would build a team this powerful on my own, but my time as a member of a high-performance team taught me many lessons that affect the way I lead my teams to and through impossible challenges today.

In this chapter we're going to focus on one of those lessons— which I call "gathering points." But before you can understand it, you need to understand what it means to win a seat in a top Vesper boat. You need to understand the unbelievable people who row in one.

EMOTION IN ACTION:
MAKING THE TOP BOAT

Vesper has multiple teams, and it's not shy about how they are ranked. Better rowers row in better boats. Period. This is measured primarily through tests like seat racing and other performance benchmarks throughout the year.

First, there's the summer squad. This group of hopefuls comes out for a three-month burst in the hopes of impressing Michiel and the other coaches. If they're successful, they have the chance to make one of the year-round teams. These are the boats that actually row in regattas and keep Vesper's trophy room consistently well stocked.

Of the year-round teams there's one men's and one women's boat for the eight best rowers of either gender. That's the top boat. Above the top boat is the Olympic training team, which practices separately from the rest of Vesper. The crews of the top boats are seen as the best of the best, and they earn their respect.

At Vesper, we all had to row two 2,000-meter and two 6,000-meter tests a year. Your times from these tests serve as a sort of batting average for your season. These numbers broadcast exactly how well you're doing to you, the coaches, and every single one of your teammates. Rowing is not a sport for shy people.

A good time for an elite rower on the 2k test is anything under 6:10. My best time ever at Vesper was 6:08. Only a handful of people on the planet can get under 6:00. Jaime Velez was one of them.

Jaime was the captain of the top male boat at Vesper for my entire run with the club. He wasn't just big, he wasn't just strong, he wasn't just fast, he was perfect. Which was great news for our team but bad news for someone like me who wanted to earn his own seat alongside him. Because making that seat is even harder than you might think.

In a rowing shell you have port and starboard side positions. Every rower performs better on one or the other. This means that even though there are eight seats to gun for in the top boat, only half of them favor your most powerful side. So now you're down to four seats that you might realistically have a shot at, and when a guy like Jaime already has one of them, you may as well just call it three. Or, because right behind Jaime was Mark Vorjees, two.

Mark is six foot eight. Even for rowers that's tall. And even for Vesper Mark was beyond incredible on the water. With him and Jaime leading the top boat, my chances of getting a spot on either side had gone from poor to abysmal. These aren't the type of guys you beat. They're the type of guys you respect, preferably from a safe distance.

The reason I'm explaining all this is so that you can understand how low the odds were on what I was trying to achieve. But the fact that I achieved it shouldn't make you impressed with me; it should show you how powerful leveraging human emotion can be and the results that it can accomplish.

I didn't row my way into the top boat with guys like Jamie and Mark because I got fast enough or strong enough to get the job done. I absolutely improved physically, but, more importantly, I improved emotionally as well. I got to a point at Vesper where the best guys on the team didn't just like the idea of rowing with me; they were going out of their way to make it happen. This didn't happen in the gym or on the water. It happened at the bar or at dinner or late at night in the boathouse.

If all I did at Vesper was row, I never would have made the top boat. But because they cared about me, the other elites I needed to get me where I wanted to go were on my side. They pulled hard for me in every single seat race. Not because they thought I'd be a good strategic addition to the team but because I was their friend. In short, their emotions were engaged, not just their talents. And that makes all the difference in the world.

Human beings and their emotions cannot be tricked. Effort can be faked. Talent can be faked. But emotion cannot. You can never give to someone whom you don't care about what you will to someone whom you do care about.

Even if you harp about how your team is a "family," you'll still fail to forge these connections. Emotional connections cannot be commanded; they have to be built. They are thick, knotty ropes, and each rope is composed of thousands of individual connections.

As a leader, you are responsible for creating and sustaining each of these connections one by one. The purpose of a leader on a team that wants to be exceptional has very little to do with coming up with creative strategies or good project management systems. Those are just the table stakes. If you want to be a high-performance leader, then your real goal has to be creating as many emotional ties as possible to bind your team together. Teams like that don't need to be told to stay late or come in early, or to do what is necessary to hit their goals.

Teams like that do those things because you as a leader have connected them to something greater and lashed them together with so many connections that they are no longer working to get that something greater themselves. They're working to get it for the teammates they care so much about.

The bad news is that the work of creating emotional connections is not easy. The good news is that it has nothing to do with trust falls or other trust-building exercises. The actual solution can be summed up by a basic rowing technique that rowers all learn the first time they ever step in a boat. They're called "gathering points."

LEADERSHIP LESSON: ESTABLISH GATHERING POINTS

In rowing, the team that rows the best together will be the fastest boat. That's not hyperbole; it's physics.

If one of the blades goes in the water even a microsecond late or early, the boat will experience tilts, turns, and drag. The boat that wins a race is the one that makes the fewest of these mistakes. To attack these mistakes, rowers are taught to focus on gathering points.

Gathering points are the places in the stroke where you are expected to check your alignment to make sure it's in line with that of the rest of the team. They are also a chance to get back into alignment if you've started to fall off the pace.

The first gathering point is right before the blade goes in the water. We call this "the catch." The other is when the blade exits the water. We call this "the finish." At every catch and every finish you should be in perfect sync with the rower immediately in front of you. If you aren't, you need to fix it. Fast.

This strategy is simple enough, but as you progress as a rower you realize something. There aren't just two gathering points in your stroke. There are hundreds, thousands, an infinite number of moments when you could be checking on your alignment and fixing it if it's broken. You start seeing gathering points everywhere during the race. You feel them in every stroke you take.

This is the difference between an elite rower and a sufficient rower. It's also the difference between teams that meet expectations and those that surpass them. Because, just like a rowing stroke, there are infinite moments when your team can create alignment. But there are also infinite moments when it can lose that alignment.

The Monday meeting or occasional coffee break cannot be the only places you gather. Alignment, ultimately, has to come from gathering points. If you want your team to be high performance, you need to train each member of the team to recognize and take advantage of gathering points on a daily basis.

Here is an example. One member of your team has been working on a project for three months. It has a very large scope, and you and the leadership of your organization have prioritized it. But as the teammate continues to work, she realizes there is way too much work for her to do on her own, the deadline is far too tight, and the deliverables were never all that clear to begin with.

This teammate is not particularly outspoken. She works very hard but isn't one to speak up in meetings or create friction. So she just keeps plugging away on the project alone. She's hitting her milestones for now, but a disaster is brewing in the near future.

Finally, she realizes that she can't make the deadline on her own, so she grabs one of her teammates and asks if he can help on this one part of the project. He agrees but doesn't really understand what the finish line is for this project, what the steps are, and how their work will actually make an impact for themselves and the wider team.

The original project owner pulls in a few more teammates to assist her, or maybe her new recruit does some recruiting of his own, but the same problems persist. Before long, you have a team full of people working on a project they don't understand and aren't executing very well. The deadline is still too tight. They still aren't going to make it.

This is a team that has missed gathering points, a lot of them. There was an opportunity to gather when this project was first launched so that everyone could understand what was being built, why it was being built, and what work they may be responsible for. There was an opportunity to gather when the project owner noticed that the scope and timelines were way too ambitious for one person. There was an opportunity to gather when the second teammate realized he didn't really know what they were working on.

If that team was aware of and looking out for gathering points, they would have noticed something was wrong. When you're rowing competitively, you're hypersensitive to what's happening with the person in front of you. I knew Mike's back like the back of my hand by the time I left Sonoma State. I could see the hitch in his arm, watch the handle of his oar go around the fulcrum of our boat, hear his blade hit the water. I wasn't trying to copy him. I was anticipating. It's like a song you know by heart. You know what should be coming next, and you notice when something changes. If Paul McCartney starts rapping in the middle of "Paperback Writer," you should raise an eyebrow. Probably both of them.

Elite teams need to operate the same way. The key to mastering gathering points isn't to know what they all are and have a canned solution to each one. The key is just to know that they exist and to make sure that your team knows this as well. Team-size problems cannot be solved by ad hoc solutions. The only solution is to reset, realign, and lock in to a consistent, perfectly synchronized stroke. And this has to happen multiple times a day, every day, until the job is done.

Every frustrated exchange, poorly worded email, or inefficient meeting is a moment when you've missed a gathering point. If you aren't watching for gathering points and you haven't empowered your team to do the same, you'll probably miss the next one. And the next one.

The symptoms of missed gathering points in an office are the same as they are in a boat. The office starts to feel heavier. You start doing more work to go slower. And you know you're going slower because you know how fast you were going before.

Sustainability can be defined as what a team is capable of when it hits the maximum number of gathering points possible. Once you see that type of performance, it can and should become the standard for what you should be doing as a team from that point on. Anything less should be treated as a symptom of a missed gathering point and corrected immediately.

As a leader you first have to educate your team about the

reality of these gathering points and make it clear that hitting them is everyone's responsibility. High-performance teams feel comfortable about communicating. And leaders of high-performance teams foster this willingness in their people. It's not being petty for someone to tell you that John has missed the last three conference calls. It's vital. If the goal is shared, then your performance becomes my performance as well.

Too many leaders work hard to keep things from being personal on their teams. The best teams are always personal. Human emotions are the cornerstones of high performance, and leveraging them requires building connections through consistently looking for and hitting gathering points.

Business is not typically personal, but high-performance teams are. The members of these teams are completely interdependent. Only with the power of these emotional, relational bonds can your team move from adequate to exceptional.

Leaders can ensure that this happens in a variety of ways, and it's different for every team. Maybe it's improving how your office is laid out. Maybe it's seeing that Jim works from home and Angela doesn't. Maybe it's getting up and walking over to someone instead of sending an email. Maybe it's halting a project altogether until the gathering points can be hit and alignment can be restored.

Your team has an endless number of gathering points. This means your team has many chances to lose its alignment. But it also means it has just as many opportunities to get that alignment back.

No team hits all of its gathering points. But high-performance teams never stop trying to hit as many as possible. In the end the team that hits the most is the one that wins the race.

MOVING ON

One point eight seconds. That's not a lot of time. It's less than
the four years it took me to rise through the ranks at Vesper—
ultimately to be chosen for the Olympic training team. It's less
than the six years I'd spent becoming an elite rower. And it's
less than the 27 years I'd spent growing into the adult I was the
day of the Olympic trials.

But, as it turns out, 1.8 seconds was enough time for me to
miss qualifying for the Olympics.

When people find out I missed something so enormous by a
number so small, they all react the same way: with pity. They
assume it must have been the worst day of my life, that I must
not be able to watch the games on TV without putting a foot
through my Samsung, that it must have driven me away from
my friends and family and straight down a bottle of Jameson.
I do like whiskey, but that's because it's delicious.

I can't say that I enjoyed the experience, but I can say
that it was definitely the second-best outcome I could have
accomplished.

The reality is that failing to make the Olympics, for any
athlete, means waiting for four years to try again. For me,
that would mean another four years at Vesper. Another four
years of putting my career (Vesper rowers do not get paid), my
relationships, and my future plans on pause.

If I had lost the trials by 10 seconds, I probably would have
tried again. I would know I could have done better, and I
wouldn't be able to rest until everyone else knew it too. But
the truth is, I think losing by 1.8 seconds was the best I could
possibly do.

Like I said before, it's okay to quit when you realize that a goal isn't worth the sacrifice and suffering required to reach it. What isn't okay is never finding one that is.

In much the same way I realized back in college that I was not going to become a major league pitcher, I now had to admit that I was not going to become an Olympic rower either. I knew the Olympics was no longer the goal for me.

But I was about to find the goal that was.

GATHERING POINT: INFINITE ALIGNMENT

» **Gathering points:** Gathering points are opportunities for a team to realign itself toward its stated goals and/or toward one another. The more gathering points a team has, the better chance it has to become high performance and remain high performance.

» **Opportunity is everywhere:** Gathering points can be formal (a sit-down meeting) or informal (a walk to your team member's desk to see how her weekend went, or how her kid is doing). There are an infinite number of these opportunities to realign.

» **Business is personal:** High-performance teams are hyper-sensitive to one another's interests. It's a personal relationship. Business isn't usually personal, but the members of high-performance teams understand that they are, and must be, completely dependent on one another.

FOUR QUESTIONS

I had gone from a washed-out baseball player to a struggling rower to an elite Vesper assassin to nearly qualifying for the Olympics. But now, the time had come to test my mettle against my most serious challenge yet: the art of the perfect latte.

As it turns out, regatta trophies don't take you quite as far in the job market as I'd hoped. Most respectable companies choose instead to focus on stupid things like "skills" or "experience." That's companies for you.

After Vesper, the only job I could get in a hurry was at a Peet's Coffee near where I grew up. Every morning, faithful patrons would stream into Peet's to grab a morning jolt and see what happens when you cram a six foot four rower into a small kitchen surrounded by hot liquids.

Skidding so suddenly from the highest levels of athleticism to the lowest levels of hot bean water preparation gave me a nasty case of professional whiplash. I had decided to forgo another four years of Olympic training, but I never thought I would be this far removed from the forces of competition that fuel my psyche.

I tried my best to bring some elite thinking to the good people of Peet's, but my coworkers quickly tired of me shouting out my victory every time I completed a drink in half the time allotted by the manual. This wasn't working out.

I won't bore you with every step on my Holden Caulfield

journey for purpose as a young, Vesper-less adult. But after being cast out of the barista life, I managed to bluff my way into a few higher-profile jobs and eventually landed at a professional development firm.

This company dispatched me all over the country to help struggling CEOs get better results out of their struggling teams. That job sowed the seeds for what would eventually become a company of my own, but all the time it was significant for two reasons.

When we look back on our lives, we tend to boil entire years down to one or two major outcomes. We reduce our entire childhoods to the same five or six anecdotes. You might say that high school was amazing because you met your wife. Your first job mattered because it led to that better one.

That sounds depressing, but it should actually excite you. Every phase of your life will have a least one major impact on the next step in your journey. Nothing is ever wasted. For me, this phase of life would be defined by one decision I made and one person I met. Let's start with the decision.

THE GOAL

The Talisker Whiskey Atlantic Challenge. The idea for an Atlantic rowing race was conceived in 1997 by Sir Chay Blyth. Since then, the race has bounced around between a few different owners and changed names a few times. In 2012 the race was purchased by Atlantic Campaigns SL, which found a sponsor in the Scottish spirits company Talisker. The race's official name is The Talisker Whiskey Atlantic Challenge—the World's Toughest Row.

In my circles it's called something else: The World's Most Impossible Race.

Once a year, teams from around the world compete to cross more than 3,000 miles of open ocean in single-, two-, four-, and eight-person boats. More people have been in space than have completed the Talisker. But finishing is one thing. Winning is another.

To win this race you have to keep your boat moving at all times. That doesn't sound too hard until you remember what's powering it: you. This is a rowing race, so no sails, no motor, nothing but you, your teammates, and the ocean.

To keep pace, most crews embrace the two-hours-on-two-hours-off system. That means you're sleeping for two hours, rowing for two hours, and repeating that pattern until the race is over. That adds up to 12 hours of the toughest rowing possible every single day until the race is finished, which can take well over a month. And that's when everything's going your way.

If the wind stops blowing, if there's a storm, if one of your teammates gets hurt, your task gets even more insane. Then you need to row 18 hours a day with only four hours of intermittent sleep sprinkled sparingly throughout. For Talisker rowers, hallucinations, disembodied voices, and detailed conversations with the cast of *Frasier* are par for the course.

Each member of the team is allotted a carefully controlled five liters of water a day. Not exactly a doctor-recommended hydration plan. And this water isn't just for drinking. It's also for your food.

Race rules state that each boat must carry 5,000 calories worth of food per person per day for at least 60 days. In a competition where every ounce counts, that's a lot of weight. Welcome to the wonderful world of freeze-dried food. You haven't lived until you've torn open a pouch of desiccated beef stroganoff, mixed it with two ounces of the only thing keeping you alive, stirred it half-heartedly, and felt that telltale crunch as you chomped down on each partially rehydrated morsel. Just like mama used to make.

Competitors in the Talisker lose an average of 20 percent of their body weight. Since most of the male competitors weigh in at over 200 pounds at the starting line, that's 30 to 50 pounds shed by your body in a month. Take notes, Atkins.

And, don't forget, all these amazing experiences take place on a boat not that much larger than your average living room sectional. Four-person ocean rowing boats are roughly 30 feet long and six feet wide. They're made of fiberglass, which is light and sturdy enough to withstand the journey ahead. These boats are self-righting, meaning that if a wave flips them, they're designed to roll themselves back into a safe position. File that one under Cool Features You Never Want to Use.

These four-person boats typically have two cabins—a larger one in the stern and a smaller one in the bow. By "cabin" I mean tiny metal caves that can sleep one rower very uncomfortably or two if they agree to get married first.

The first thing most people ask after finding out all this is "why?" Why would any rational adult leave friends, family, and career for an entire month (or much more if you take into account training time), to do something so incredibly dangerous, inhumanly uncomfortable, and obviously unnecessary?

Is there a huge cash prize for winning? No. Does a victory automatically get you a spot on an Olympic team? No. Is there some sort of sea monster you've all been hired by the government to try and kill? We're not supposed to talk about that.

Why? is the question of the hour. Why did Alex Honnold

climb 3,000 feet up the face of El Capitan without a rope to catch him if he fell? Why did James Tabor descend 7,000 feet into the earth exploring the Krubera Cave in the Republic of Georgia? Why did three wonderful men with children strap themselves into a rocket that launched them to the moon? Why do adventurers go on adventures?

The answer is more practical than you might think, and it has nothing to do with poorly developed brains or daddy issues. The reason adventurers are able to identify these apparently insane directives and motivate themselves to finish is because adventurers have a system for choosing the right goals.

I'm about to teach it to you.

LEADERSHIP LESSON:
FOUR QUESTIONS TO ASK YOUR GOALS

I discovered the Talisker in the most boring way possible. I didn't hear the legend from some old sea dog at the bar or discover a map to the finish line in a clamshell on the beach. I googled it.

One day I was in my apartment after a long stint of traveling for my company. I enjoyed my job. I was starting to hit respectable levels of real, adult success. But something was missing.

You might call this "the call of the wild." A millennial would call it "chasing my bliss." But I call it "disappointment." Not in myself, but in the challenges I was tackling. None of them felt right for my skills, my opportunities, and my ambitions. So I decided to ask four questions that would hopefully help me identify one that was.

Question One:
Is this goal worthy of me?

This is the first and most important thing anyone can and should demand of their goals. It also happens to be the question most people never even think of. We ask ourselves so many questions about a goal before we ever even consider this one.

How much money will I make? Where do I have to live to pull this off? How much money will I make? What will my office look like? How much money will I make? These aren't bad questions. They just shouldn't be your first questions.

The concept of worthiness has gone out of fashion. The idea is basically this: some goals are simply not big enough for the effort you're going to give to them. When you're triaging potential goals, you need to start here. But what does assessing a goal's "worth" even look like? There's a useful subprocess that you can use to answer this larger question.

Check Your Glory

Every goal has its own glory, and it's important to be picky about the ones you want. You wouldn't hire someone at work who didn't match a job description. So create a job description for your goal.

How many years do you want it to take? What sort of experiences would you like it to offer? What skills would you like to use in achieving it? Once you build out this job posting for the goal, you can start auditioning goals to see which one fits.

The first thing you should check on each goal's CV is this: what glory is it offering? Say you're an executive manager now, but do you even like your company? You got into a top med school, but are you sure that a doctor's life is what's driving you? You're dating a guy who would probably marry you, but he eats his peas one at a time.

Knowing which glory a goal offers is a matter of looking past its appearance to see where it ends. If you can put your eyes on that, and if you've taken the time to formulate a job description that any goal has to meet, then finding a goal worthy of you stops being ambiguous and starts being practical.

Question Two:
What are the limits?

Growing up, most of us had parents who said things like "You can be anything when you grow up!"

That's an example of terrible motivation. Sorry, Mom. In a world where every decision is equally viable, nothing can reasonably be chosen. That's why constraint is a decision maker's best friend. What you won't do will point you more clearly to what you should do.

All of us have lines we simply refuse to cross. Some people will tell you that those lines are holding you back, but I think they are essential tools for crafting good decisions.

One of my lines was a beautiful California ballerina named Amelia. The two of us were speeding happily toward marriage during the time I was researching new goals, and I was completely unwilling to choose one that would take me farther from her than was absolutely necessary. Many of the goals I considered during this period would have required me to move to different countries. They went straight into the No column.

It's much easier to farm the 100 acres you've put a fence around than it is to plant corn across the entire planet. Put up boundaries early in the goal-setting process, and what follows will proceed with far more clarity, efficiency, and sanity.

Question Three:
Is this goal realistic?

It may seem odd to start talking about realism in a book about rowing across the ocean, but this question is another key safeguard that prevents you from choosing the wrong goal.

Realistic here does not mean simple. It does not mean risk-free. It does not mean predictable. It doesn't even mean possible. *Realistic* in this context means that this goal can be completed, by you, in this lifetime. It has nothing to do with asking whether or not it will be easy. It means asking yourself if you were built to make this thing happen.

Barack Obama was built to become president. So was Donald Trump. Now that I've offended everyone, let me explain. Both of those men had exactly the right tools in their kits to successfully carve a tunnel through the morass that is a presidential election.

Obama and Trump were built for different times and would be embraced by those with different sentiments, but both of them could look at a goal like becoming president and say with confidence, "That is realistic for me personally."

Pursuing a goal that's realistic means doing an audit of yourself and then doing a stress test of the goal. What qualities does this goal demand? Do you have those qualities? If not, move on. As someone who should never ski black diamonds but does, I can guarantee that only disaster awaits when you pick the wrong path.

Question Four:
Will my passion carry me through?

You may find that even the most worthy goal is hard to care about when you're halfway through it. You must choose a goal that you can see yourself pursuing day in and day out for as long as it takes.

For example, as soon as they find out I'm a professional adventurer, everyone always asks me if I'm going to climb Mount Everest. I have some major problems with the entire Mount Everest industrial complex, but, aside from that, it still wouldn't be a good goal for me.

I'm tall, broad, and built for difficult, repetitive actions over a long period. Rowing, hiking, cross-country skiing, binging *The Office*—these are my things. To climb Everest I'd have to restructure my entire mind and rebuild my entire body. The diet and training it would take to accomplish it doesn't sound impossible to me, but they do sound like hell.

I'm okay with pain. I've built a career out of enduring pain, but it's my pain. When we talk about passion, what we're really talking about are things we're willing to do even when they cost us something. Even when it hurts.

Can you stay up until 4 a.m. building PowerPoints? Can you speak in front of 4,000 people without throwing up beforehand? Do you live for helping people with their personal problems even when the problems are extremely difficult?

Everyone has a pain they can take. Find yours, and you'll find your passion, and that will lead you to your goal.

THE PROCESS IN ACTION

I knew I was going to race the Talisker. I had sent the coal of possibility through the fiery furnace of the process above. Then I held in my hand an indestructible diamond of purpose. But the man across from me was the one who had to buy it.

By the time I got to Chris Coke, I had been rejected by Nike, Under Armour, all the major athletic players. None of them wanted to shell out more than $150,000 to sponsor an athlete they'd never heard of in a sport very few 18- to 35-year-olds care about. But where these companies saw an uncompelling request on a very large stack, Chris saw a perfect fit.

Chris is the CEO of Carlisle Companies, and in this case I was the goal he had to evaluate. Was I worthy? Was I realistic? Was I in line with his passion? Executing my dream meant that I would be his dream.

The Carlisle sponsorship is an example of goal setting done right. It didn't make as much direct business sense for him to sponsor my boat as it did for Nike or Adidas, but Chris was interested in something more than the obvious.

Chris is a leader through and through. He has more than 15,000 employees, and most of them work hard days in busy factories. That's a lot of people looking to you to make sure that their tables are full and their 401(k) contributions are matched. Chris feels that pressure and uses it to select better goals.

After our contract was signed, Chris looked at me and said point-blank that he wasn't doing this to sell more products. He was doing it to reach his people: To show them that their company believes in something beyond the machinery they create. To inspire them to set big goals. To prove that he would support them if they did that.

He was fulfilling a piece of advice that my friend John Cady, head of business education for the Kelley School of Business at Indiana University, told me when I started to hit brick walls in my search for funds.

He told me to pursue people who shared my values, not my industry. And that's my advice to you as you go out and start setting goals. Once you pick a goal, share it with the people who will push for it just as hard as you will, if not harder.

That's exactly what I was going to do next. I had a goal. I had a sponsor. Now all I needed was a team.

GATHERING POINT:
INTERROGATE YOUR GOALS

≫ **High-performance goals:** When setting a goal, ask yourself a set of questions. These questions are designed to build the focus and confidence you will need when the suffering and sacrifice starts to kick in. They are also designed to ensure that you are being efficient with your time.

≫ Question One: Is this goal worthy of me?

≫ Question Two: What are the limits? How far am I willing to go, and what am I willing to do?

≫ Question Three: Is this goal realistic? Knowing myself and my capabilities, is this goal realistic for me to achieve?

≫ Question Four: Will my passion carry me through? Said another way, is this something I really want?

BEYOND MOTIVATION

Booking.com is one of my sponsors. My favorite thing about the company is the way they build their physical workplaces. Booking has more than a dozen offices around the world. I've visited several of them, and no matter which one I'm in they are all instantly recognizable as a Booking office.

The offices don't look identical—each uses the culture of its home country to add a unique spin—but they do all feel identical. Any one of their employees could fly from Amsterdam to New York, swipe their keycard, and instantly be in a familiar, comforting, energizing space. They can go from being strangers in a strange land to being in the comforts of their own "corporate home."

To me, being able to provide this kind of ambient inclusion for a team is a strong step on the path to high performance. A large number of Booking employees stay at the company for an unusually long time. In my opinion, that's because of the culture.

Teams need to be on the same page in order to execute, and this usually means going a lot further than holding regular staff meetings on Wednesdays. Teams cannot be just a collection of talented individuals. They need to be fused together into something much more powerful.

I learned that the hard way.

THE BOAT

The starting line for the Talisker is in the beautiful town of La Gomera on the island of San Sebastian in the Canary Islands. It's more than 5,500 miles from my home in California, but it was starting to feel painfully close as the days ticked by. I had less than a year to prepare for the race of a lifetime.

I knew the training would be difficult. I had already bid a sad farewell to sugar, gluten, and alcohol. I had upped my workouts to eight a week, taking only Sundays off to rest and stare at the ice cream I could no longer eat.

I had discipline to spare, but what I didn't have was a boat. Fortunately, the rowing world is tight. I asked around and eventually found my way to Rannoch Adventure—a British company that specializes in the creation, maintenance, and stocking of ocean-ready rowboats.

Fresh off my successful sponsorship meeting with Carlisle, I put a call in to Rannoch. The voice on the other end of the line sounded like a cross between Russell Crowe and Idris Elba— the exact voice you want the guy building your boat to have.

That glorious baritone belonged to Angus Collins, who would be happy to build our team a boat (for a reasonable six-figure sum, of course). All he needed was a name to put on the side.

And I knew exactly which one to choose.

THE TEAM

Recruiting for a race like the Talisker is easier than you might think, but recruiting well is another story. I had three rules for who I would pick to crew this race. The first: make sure the people I put in the boat at the start of the race are able to walk out onto the dock in Antigua at the finish.

There's no shortage of weekend warriors who think that rowing across the Atlantic can't be much harder than the Tough Mudder they ran last July. More than a few of these guys reached out to me when word of my plans started to get around my small suburban community.

What I told them was thanks but no thanks. What I wanted to tell them was that every boat in the Talisker has to set sail with a body bag, and I'd rather not have to put them in it.

The second rule I followed was that all my rowers had to be American.

This wasn't part of some far-right mission to Make America Row Again. This was about putting together the team that could generate the most glory. At the time I was recruiting, no American team had ever won the Talisker. Historically, the European teams have kicked our asses. Recruiting European athletes would give us a better chance to finish well, but the allure of captaining the first American team to win this race was too powerful to pass up.

Which brings me to my third rule: rowers in my boat wouldn't be there to finish; they would be there to win.

As incredible a feat as it is, finishing the Talisker wasn't a goal I considered worthy of myself. Maybe it was coming up short for the Olympics, maybe it was never winning a national championship at Sonoma State, or maybe it was not getting that puppy for my sixth birthday. Whatever it was, for once I didn't just want to be good. I didn't just want to be elite. I wanted to be the undisputed champion of the world.

At this point in my life, I felt like I was constantly looking at a wall full of silver medals. The Talisker was my chance to go for the gold, but I couldn't do it alone.

Nick

For a race like this, every boat needs an engine, a person so strong and so consistent that he can pick up the slack of the smaller, lighter crew members if need be.

I met Nick Kahn when we were rowing for different teams on Boathouse Row. Even among rowers, Nick is a beast. He's the kind of guy who makes you say, "Oh, shit!" when you see him in the boat you have to beat.

Nick is six foot five inches and 225 pounds of pure power. Back in his Philly days, he had rowed to great success for both Temple University and Undine Barge Club. He was living in Pittsburgh working for Google. He was also at the top off my call list for potential Talisker teammates.

I've never known Nick to back away from a challenge, and this was no exception. After one phone call, he was in. His why matched my own: We were agreed. We weren't entering this race. We were winning it.

One down. Two to go.

Ethan

Ocean rowing is a master class in Murphy's law. At some point, everything that can go wrong will go wrong. Formulating a strategic route and a strong game plan at the beginning is important, but when the wind shifts or the ocean decides it's had enough of you, you need something better than a plan. You need a fixer.

Ethan Davis had a reputation for solving problems. I had worked with him on more than a few leadership programs for my day job, and he'd earned my respect for his ability to think quickly and act decisively in a crisis.

On top of that, as the head of the Greater Houston Rowing Club, Ethan was no slouch behind the oars, either. He wasn't as big as Nick or even me, but he was strong. As a trustworthy fixer who was light enough not to slow us down and powerful enough to keep us moving, Ethan offered our boat some much-needed utility.

Ethan sought me out when he heard about the race. I like people who take initiative, and after a few weeks of questioning and contemplation, he committed himself to the team.

Three seats out of four were now filled with traditional, experienced rowers. I could easily have filled the final spot with another of the same. But where's the fun in that?

Tom

More than a few people whom I consider friends asked to join the team. These weren't just thrill seekers, either. They were big, strong, successful rowers. But for one reason or another, I had to turn them away. All except one.

Tom Magarov has sharp, dark features—a product of his Eastern European heritage. He worked for the same leadership firm as I did, and together we had organized and executed events on almost every continent.

Tom and I have run on the Great Wall of China. We've swum with sharks in Thailand, ridden camels in Oman, and drunk ourselves silly in Bavarian beer gardens. We've talked, we've laughed, and we've shared stories. We were, and are, tremendous friends, but he wasn't on my radar to crew an ocean row.

He's tall—six foot four to be exact, the same height as me—but he's skinny. Even though he eats well and exercises religiously, mass just seems to avoid him the way I avoid any music released after 1995. He had some rowing experience, but he wasn't someone I planned on asking to join the team. Then I heard his why.

Tom grew up in Azerbaijan with his mother and younger brother back when it was still a Soviet Socialist Republic. His mother took good care of her two children, but he can still remember waiting in line for bread while watching the tanks roll by.

Eventually, his whole family moved to Denver so that Tom could wash cars and put himself through college. Years later, he had a well-paying job, his mother had become a successful nurse, and his brother had just graduated with a degree in finance and great career prospects.

Even before they moved, Tom had loved America. His dream was to move here and live the life he had grown up watching on television. Now that he was here, he had a new dream.

He wanted to say thank-you to the land that had embraced him so richly. He wanted to become a champion for his adopted home. He wanted to give it something it had never had before: a win in the Talisker Atlantic Challenge.

Of all of us, Tom was the weakest from both a rowing and purely physical perspective. But his why was just as strong as, if not stronger than, my own.

I'm a map nerd. I took a look at the coordinates for each of our hometowns and averaged the latitudes of each one. Once again, putting my college degree to good use. To my surprise, I arrived at a nice round number. Our team was complete. And then, we had our name. Latitude 35 was born. We could win; we would win. I was sure of it; I was convinced of it.

I was wrong.

LEADERSHIP LESSON:
MEASURE THE CHANGE

Due to the circumstances vividly described in the next chapter, this version of Latitude 35 was not bound for victory. At least not the victory we had in mind.

Some of those circumstances were out of my control as a leader, but not all of them. The most serious mistake I made was thinking that strong rowers would automatically become a strong team, that just sharing the same space and the same heading would make us a team.

Recruiting is like gambling. You do your best to make an informed choice, but ultimately the end result is often out of your control. A brainiac from MIT can win that control back by using formulas and statistics. Leaders have a tool to do this as well. It's called motivation.

Motivation is the process by which a leader shepherds one or more individuals toward a common goal. This means different things to different leaders. Some try to motivate through fear, others through friendship, and still others through offers of opportunity. But I have yet to meet a leader who understands motivation the same way I do after taking this original Latitude 35 team out onto the open ocean.

What I learned out there is that emotion is not a practice; it's a process. What most leaders call "motivation" I call "step one." And it's a relatively simple step.

Every person gets inspired by one of six motivators: time, money, security, challenge, purpose, or positivity. Here's how they are defined:

»» Time: The possibility of creating more agency for yourself

»» Money: The possibility of earning a larger income. Managers need to stop acting like money is only a bonus. People like money, and they usually want more of it. Some want it more than others, and these are the people who are most powerfully motivated by the possibility of earning a larger income.

»» Security: The possibility of eliminating anxieties.

»» Challenge: The possibility of becoming a better person.

»» Purpose: The possibility of creating a better world for other people.

»» Positivity: The possibility of being in and adding to a welcoming, encouraging, and uplifting environment.

Everyone's mind at work will be most directed toward one of these things. But that doesn't mean the others are not valuable. Too many leaders try to slot their teammates into simple boxes. Dan is only in this for the money. Tanya is the optimist of the group. Carl likes his time off.

But, in reality people are beings of nuance. They ebb and flow, they alter their course, they change. The way you as a leader can go beyond "motivation" and push toward high performance is to become aware of those changes and measure them.

Do this exercise with your teammates: have each of them take those six motivators and order them on a piece of paper from most to least important. This gradient will be a much more powerful guide for you as a leader than a simple statement "I'd like to be promoted by the end of the year."

It will also likely help your teammates become more attuned to their own mind-set, passions, and reasons for being in their job in the first place. As a leader, you cannot rely only on intuition or your own observations to decipher what is driving your teammates. This process is too important to be subtle. If you want a high-performance team, you need each team member to know what they're doing and why they're doing it. And you need to know that as well. Which leads to the next step in the process.

If you were an average leader, you would stop as soon as you realized your teammate wanted more money. You would divert energy to putting that person on a path to more money and pat yourself on the back for a job well done. That strategy will work, but only up to a point. Even understanding a teammate's full motivational spectrum will not give you all the information you need to understand and motivate them properly. That ability can be mastered only when you go beyond typical motivation and start measuring the change.

You have to repeat the gradient exercise at least once a year, if not more. You will find that the results are fascinating. Teammates who said they were most interested in getting more free time for themselves will suddenly be more interested in money, or vice versa. By capturing that change, you will inevitably ask yourself the question *why?* and the answer will be the overarching why that is driving that teammate.

Most of us can understand our own whys, but this process allows you to diagnose the whys of other people. The reason your teammate who was interested in time is now interested in money is because she got engaged last month and is eager to start saving for a down payment on a house. If you don't take her through this spectrum more than once, you may be going out of your way to get her more vacation days when what she really wants is to be in the office working overtime.

You might think that motivation is something you do, when really it's a collection of many things that you keep doing over time. People are constantly evolving, so as a high-performance leader you need to make it your mission to become obsessed with those evolutions. Those changes will reveal who your teammates really are and what they truly care about.

Once you have that understanding, you can begin to make the decisions and take the actions that leverage those teammates' emotions and make the best use of the gathering points you provide for them.

In building the first Latitude 35 team, I didn't map out these motivational spectrums or take the time it required to truly understand the whys of my team.

That was a mistake. A mistake that almost cost us all our lives.

THE STARTING LINE

Aside from my wife, there's only one "she" I would ever call truly beautiful. Except this she is made out of carbon fiber and infused with a healthy splash of optimism.

True to his reputation, Angus built our team an incredible boat. Everything from her colors to her state-of-the-art design to her name was a testament to the purpose of our team. She was *American Spirit*, and she was ready to row. And, after two years of training, so were we.

Nick, Tom, Ethan, and I had spent the last two weeks in La Gomera getting to know the other racers and preparing to launch. As we strapped ourselves in behind our oars, I couldn't help thinking about my dad.

When I was a kid, he set up a simple net between two trees in our front yard. He walked 30 paces away and dropped a bucket of baseballs. If I really wanted to be a pitcher, I had to empty that bucket as many times as I could against that net every day. And I did.

This, I thought, would be no different. An ocean to cross is just like a bucket to empty. You can throw only one ball at a time. You can take only one stroke on the oars at a time. That, as my dad would say, is the key to becoming a champion.

I was torn out of this warm reverie by the sharp crack of a starting pistol and the thunderous roar of the spectators. My legs surged, my back engaged, and the *American Spirit* erupted toward the open ocean.

The race was on.

GATHERING POINT:
MEASURE THE CHANGE

>> **Ask the questions:** You must properly assess your team members' motivations.

>> **Study the gradients:** You should know that these motivations will change as each team member advances in their career and personal life. What was once their number one motivator may not be a factor at all a year later in driving them to be more productive.

>> **Act on the results:** Your job as a leader is not to judge an individual's motivations. Your only task is to learn their true motivators by understanding their gradient and how it changes over time. Then you can create a path that gets them those things while simultaneously pursuing your team's larger goal.

CELEBRATE CONNECTION

Seasickness happens because your body and brain have stopped getting along. On a boat, your body starts capturing the natural sensations that occur once you start bobbing up and down on the swells. However, your brain doesn't like focusing on things like that. It tries its best to erase the motion from your awareness so you can focus on other, more important, things. Neither brain nor body communicates this very well to the other, so your eyes, inner ears, and stomach all get caught in a nasty feedback loop.

Cue the retching.

If you've ever taken a cruise, you know that they keep a healthy supply of Dramamine packs on board at all times. They do this because even people who have never experienced a moment of motion-induced nausea before in their lives can be reduced to a vomiting, sobbing mass as soon as the boat leaves the harbor. And that's on a 200,000-ton Carnival Cruise Line ship. Imagine what could happen on a boat that weighs less than a Prius.

Every ocean rower experiences some form of seasickness. It's impossible to avoid. For some competitors this is a small annoyance that they can shrug off with a swig of water or a few hours' rest. For others it can be completely debilitating or even deadly. Unfortunately for Latitude 35, Nick was trending hard toward the latter condition.

We had been in La Gomera for two weeks prepping our boat,

checking our gear, and, most importantly, taking the *American Spirit* on a handful of important practice jaunts around the harbor. On each of these rows Nick had been hit with haymaker after haymaker of seasickness that forced us to return to shore without getting a full test run under our belts.

We expected this adventure to be difficult, but we were hoping those difficulties would at least wait until the race actually started. We had reached a crossroads.

I'd like to say that I rallied the troops, pushed Nick through his pain, and won a Nobel Prize for curing seasickness. But the reality is much less ideal. We were a team, but this was not a team decision. It was Nick's, and he decided to race.

DECEMBER 2015

The Atlantic Ocean

Day 1

Rowing is a game of inches and seconds. That applies to ocean rowing as well. Every movement matters. Every decision has consequences.

As soon as we hear the crack of the gunshot through the tropical air, Latitude 35 puts its plan into action. The shortest distance between two points is a straight line, but in an ocean race, the shortest route is not necessarily the fastest. Bone-crunching currents, scorching trade winds, and varying wave conditions all need to be taken into account by teams as they plan their paths to victory.

Some teams like to start with as many rowers on the oars as they can get. Power is crucial at the start if you're trying to cannonball through the momentum of the shore waves as they roll toward land. But not all currents need to be fought.

Our plan isn't about power. It's about consistency, skill, and clever routing. We hug the shore and let the currents work with us, all the while listening closely for the telltale gunshot that will let us know another boat has launched, that another shark is in the water.

That first day is mercifully uneventful. We lock comfortably into the two-men-on-two-men-off routine that will become our life for the next month at least. As the sunlight fades to a golden brown, the team seems strong, our chances seem bright, and the Atlantic seems friendly.

But looks can be deceiving.

Day 2

The *American Spirit* slides silently past El Hierro, the final island in the Canary Islands chain. As we press on, the island's lush green peaks wink playfully under the horizon.

I don't have a good word to describe what comes next. "The Atlantic is really big," doesn't do justice to the psychic gut punch you get from that first moment on the ocean.

Usually, you're surrounded by landmarks that provide an easily digestible sense of scale. The office is right down this hall, the Starbucks is just over the hill, my dad lives 10 miles down Main Street. Simple. This certainty makes your brain very happy. It loves gathering reference points around it like a soft security blanket of predictability. As long as it can orient itself, your mind can plan your steps, advise your actions, and ensure your safety.

But the moment that the final speck of El Hierro slips out of sight, the entire world becomes water. My brain has no idea what to do about that. It has nothing to grab onto. Everything is blue and white and moving. My body is in the most open space on planet Earth, but my mind is crumbling into a paradoxical claustrophobia. We are locked inside an infinite cage.

This is the most dangerous part of ocean rowing. If your bearing is off by even a fraction of a degree, you could find yourself moving in circles for weeks until your food runs out and you die. Or you could wander accidentally into a storm system that destroys your boat and you die. Or you could get caught up in the wrong current and wind up in New Jersey instead of Antigua.

To keep on the right track in the face of unlimited possibilities, ocean boats use an autotiller. This is a mechanical arm that keeps the rudder locked on to a very specific heading so that you don't spend a day rowing in the wrong direction. Autotillers serve a vitally important purpose, but they're also like the people who comment on YouTube videos—temperamental, needy, and much more fragile than they should be.

If your autotiller breaks, which it will, you either have to replace it fast or keep your heading by hand. One man's arm against the might of an entire ocean isn't exactly a fair fight. Tilling by hand also keeps one crew member off the oars and out of bed. It's brutal. Just to be safe, we brought four autotillers.

Our autotiller was set firmly to 240—a route that would take us southwest to the strongest winds and most favorable currents. But we weren't alone. The overwhelming favorite to win that year's Talisker was the *Jean Marie*, skippered by none other than Angus Collins—the man who built the *American Spirit*.

Angus had chosen a course almost identical to ours. For the first few days we tried to keep the odds-on-favorite in sight—keep your friends close and all that. But even small discrepancies in trajectory add up on the ocean. Before the third day ended, we had lost them over the horizon. Now our only indication of how well we were doing would come from the Yellowbrick.

The Yellowbrick—named after the famous road in Oz—is a plastic-wrapped brick of electronics that consistently pings an unusually strong GPS signal back to land. If a fish got too close to the Yellowbrick and bit you, you'd probably become some sort of aquatic-themed superhero with self-esteem issues.

The signals from the Yellowbrick are fed back to the land managers and out to the public through the Talisker's official companion smartphone app. Each boat is represented by one of several multicolored arrows.

At the end of day three, our tiny yellow arrow was nearly overlapping with Angus's purple one. We were actually giving the *Jean Marie* a run for its money. I felt like we were Rocky Balboa going the distance against champion Apollo Creed.

But I was wrong. We were actually Apollo all along, and the ocean was Ivan Drago. And he must break us.

Day 5

The farther we got from land, the larger the waves became. In no time we were climbing up and down 20-foot swells. As the watery slopes grew steeper, so did the severity of Nick's seasickness.

Initially, he just needed a little more time in the cabin than the rest of us. I was in daily conference over the sat phone with race officials, who told us that time is the best medicine for seasickness. It's pretty binary, they said; either his symptoms would die down over time, or he would.

By day four Nick was barely able to keep anything in his

stomach for more than a few minutes. Precious calories and liters of fresh water were either going over the side of the *American Spirit* or, more often, onto her decks and crew members.

As Nick slipped further and further into his own personal hell, Ethan got irritable, Tom got quiet, and I got overly optimistic.

On day five I am pulled out of a sullen one-man strategy session inside my own head while on the oars by a shout from the cabin.

"Jay! JAY! Get in here!"

Tom has been in the cramped forward cabin with Nick trying to rest up for his next shift. I shoot up from my seat and stumble toward them as the *American Spirit* rockets down a massive wave.

"What is it?!" I grunt, nearly falling on top of Tom as I brace my weight on the cabin's diminutive doorframe.

"Look!" he shouts, lifting a groaning Nick out of a pool of his own vomit and onto his side. What I see will stay with me for the rest of my life. Nick's entire back is covered in bright purple sores connected by a patchwork of rapidly yellowing bruises. I like to think I'm a man of many words, but at this moment there are only two that seemed appropriate.

"Oh, . . . fuck."

Evacuation

Nick is talking to himself again. This had become a nightly occurrence as dehydration, nausea, and infection pushed him toward the edge of madness. Sometimes he talked to himself. Sometimes he spoke to invisible loved ones. But most often he talked to God. He asked God why this was happening to him.

He pleaded with God to make the pain end. He shrieked in the dead of night, begging God to take him home.

Nick has one of the sharpest athletic minds on the planet. His skill, discipline, and strength are why I recruited him in the first place. Seeing someone like that reduced to a state like this didn't just scare me. It made me question every decision I was making as captain.

To make matter worse, our losses were about to double.

I should have seen this coming. Hell, I did see this coming. But I refused to listen to anyone, even myself. And now it was time to pay for my stubbornness. The rescue boat would be taking more than one of us back to shore. Despite my attempts to convince him otherwise, Ethan had decided to leave.

I was angry. Angrier than I've ever been in my entire life. But that wasn't the issue. Anger on its own can be a good thing for adventurers. It helps you fight harder and hold on longer. But this was different. This anger had only shown up to kick in the door. And lumbering in behind it was something else. Something worse. Something dark. And so, for the first time since the Talisker filled my Google results years ago, I began to doubt.

Did I really lead a man halfway around the world just to torture him day in and day out? Could I really blame Ethan for running from something this terrifying? And, more importantly, did I actually expect that any other man would stay with me to face that terror together?

To his credit, Tom asks only for two hours to think it over. Those are the longest two hours of my life. In those two hours I have to realistically consider the possibility that everything I have believed about leadership, motivation, and elite athletics is wrong. Of everyone on my crew, Tom has the strongest why, and our years of friendship have made it possible for me to leverage his emotions more significantly than those of any of the others.

If he chooses to leave, it will be lights out for everything I've been building since Mark first found me, wounded and reeling, in the Sonoma State weight room. If he chooses to leave, I will have to face the fact that what I thought was leadership is actually just megalomania and obsession sprinkled with a dash of reckless insanity. If he chooses to leave, I won't just have failed. I will have become a failure.

Tom spends his two hours in the main cabin with the sat phone. Exactly on time the door opens, and he emerges onto the deck. Once again, his face is unreadable. I prepare myself for the worst.

"Okay, Jay," he says, "I'm in. Let's go."

I've been grateful before. I was grateful when my dad took me to a Giants game. I was grateful when Michiel took me back after I left Vesper. But this is something different. The only other time I've felt anything like this is when Amelia agreed to marry me.

That moment, like this one, featured a decision that marked a powerful emotional transaction between two people. Amelia told me she would spend the rest of her life with me. And, in a way, Tom is saying the same thing. Even if the rest of his life ends up being short, violent, and wet.

When the race was over I finally asked Tom why. Why did he decide to stay? His answer echoes in my head to this day. "It was because of you, Jay," he said. "I knew as long as you were there, everything would be okay."

With two sentences, Tom proved that the style of leadership I've built my life around is correct. No one would ever have blamed Tom for leaving. He was being given a free pass out of hell but instead chose to ride shotgun into its core. And he didn't do it because he was being led. He did it because of how connected he was to his leader.

There are so many things for the two of us to do, but the most important is finally sailing into view. The rescuers have arrived.

Anchoring a boat in the middle of the ocean is no small task. It's not like we can just drop some tattoo-like anchor with 20,000 feet of chain down to the ocean floor. With our luck we'd probably end up awakening some sort of Tokyo-destroying monster.

Instead, ocean boats have what's called a "para-anchor." This is exactly what it sounds like—a parachute that fills with water and creates enough drag to keep your boat rooted in place. Well, mostly rooted.

There really is no way to make a boat completely still on those waters. The para-anchor gets you close, but the waves still lift you, the currents still pull you, and the winds still buffet you. These motions are negligible, however. They would really be a problem only if you had to do something like catch a line of rope that's being hurled at you from another vessel.

As the rescue boat grows from a speck on the horizon to the size of a tissue box, we can clearly see that the water is far too wild for them to risk getting as close as they would like. One bad wave could send them careening into us—and, as proud a vessel as she is, the ultralight *American Spirit* would be torn to pieces by a fully equipped, motorized ocean rescue boat.

Our para-anchor is deployed, and the four of us are waiting on deck as the rescue ship attempts to wind its way between waves bigger than the house I grew up in.

The captain of the rescue boat is named Thor—like

the superhero. But I'll take this Thor over any one of the Hemsworth brothers any day of the week. Thor and I are in constant contact over the sat phone as they approach. As the waves continue to grow in strength, they finally have to settle in a little over 100 feet away from us, disappearing and reappearing as we rise and fall on opposite sides of every swell of the juggernaut waves.

We hoped we'd be able to avoid this next part but, since that is as close as they can possibly get, there is no way around it. Nick is going in the ocean.

To get him as ready as possible, we help Nick pull on his foul-weather gear—a full bodysuit of thick rubber moisture-shredding armor. He won't be winning any fashion contests, but he also won't go into shock as soon as his fever-ravaged body hits the water. Compromises.

At this distance, I can just make out Thor's powerful Nordic frame hanging off the stern of the rescue launch. I suddenly feel the familiar time-slowing sharpness that always hits me before a race at Vesper or a bottom-of-the-ninth stint on the mound. It's a feeling that means my team needs me to be the best I can possibly be. Until he is on that boat, I will do anything I can to keep Nick safe.

Ethan is another matter. He has also donned his foul-weather gear and stands staring at the means of his retreat with the same face I make every time I finally find the San Francisco side street my Uber is hiding in.

"You know, Jay," he says, "I guess years from now, when this thing's been over for a while, it will still say that all four of us finished. No matter what, all our names will be on that list."

In my younger days I was something of a brawler. I didn't take much lip from some beer-swilling frat bro at a party before connecting my fist with his face. That's not something I'm proud of, and I've worked on it. I'm down to one snide comment and two middle fingers a week.

But those words from Ethan threaten to bring the old Jason roaring back to life. It isn't just the audacity of what he said. It is how wrong he was for saying it.

In my world, the world of goals that are life-risking and take years to accomplish, no points are given for participation. It's completely binary: either you walk onto that dock in Antigua as a champion, or you don't. This clarity gets muddled back in the real world. Leaders are afraid to confidently call a spade a spade. Or, in this case, to call a weakness a weakness. When someone owns their weakness, that's when they start to improve.

But if you have someone who's content to sign their name on an A+ paper they had nothing to do with, that should be grounds for an instant dismissal. I would rather have someone on my staff lose 10 clients with honest effort than gain 10 they don't deserve. It's a simple practice that will serve you well. Give credit where credit is due, but don't be afraid to take it away just as easily.

That's why I tell Ethan to his face on the deck of the *American Spirit* that he is dead wrong. No account of this race will ever say that four men rowed this boat to the end. It will say that four started, one was taken, and another gave up. I am going to make sure of that.

Quitting is allowed. Quitting, when done correctly, is intelligent, beneficial, and intentional. Giving up, however, gets you no glory. Swinging from one vine to the next can get you through the jungle of life, but letting go will send you splattering onto the ground below.

Ethan is seething and ready to retaliate, but his retort will have to wait. The sat phone crackles to life. They are ready to evacuate.

Thor has managed to close the distance between our two boats to just 30 feet. He throws the line, but every inch of the ocean between us is raging, and I miss it. In the time it takes the line to travel from his hand toward me, a series of nasty waves drop the *American Spirit* too low for me to reach it. It sails 20 feet past me, piercing the Atlantic with the weighted rod on its end.

"Next time!" I call through the wind and spray to Thor, only then realizing that Tom has his arms wrapped tightly around my waist, saving me from going in the water instead of Nick. Every team needs a Tom.

Thor retrieves the line and coils it back into his throwing position. In the split second before his next attempt, we lock eyes. This is it.

Thor lets the line fly, harder and faster this time, and with much less loft. With the benefit of Tom's grip, I am able to reach just far enough into the expanse to wrap two fingers around the rapidly unspooling lifeline. I've never been so grateful for my freakishly long arms.

We have the line, but this is where the real danger begins. We are now tethered to the rescue boat, and at any moment the ocean could take us in opposite directions. Whatever is holding onto that line would be launched into oblivion. In this case, that's me.

"HURRY!" Thor bellows from the bottom of a wave, 20 feet below me.

Since he is healthier, Ethan takes the line first. He leaps into the water, and Thor manages to pull him through the foam without incident. Thor returns the line just as easily to my waiting hands.

Without wasting a moment, Tom and I attach the line tightly around Nick's waist. He is already trembling from the exertion of standing for so long.

"ARE YOU READY?!" I yell to Nick, hoping to spark some alertness back into his misty eyes. He nods weakly and flashes a half-hearted thumbs up. I signal to Thor and help Nick position himself on the edge of the *American Spirit*.

Before he jumps, he looks back at the two of us. "I'm so sorry," he says. "I'm so sorry to be leaving you and Tom. This is my worst nightmare."

"You don't have a damn thing to be sorry about," I assure him. "Not a damn thing."

Three. Two. One. He jumps. As soon as he hits the water, we know something is wrong. He isn't swimming, and he isn't moving closer to the rescue boat as Thor pulls on the line.

"MY FOOT!" he shouts as his mouth finally breaks through the surface of the waves. The line is wrapped around his foot. If he doesn't do something, it could pull tight enough to create a very quick, and very unnecessary, boatside amputation. We have to cut the line.

I scramble for the deck knife and, in one of the stupidest moments of my life, throw it to Tom instead of handing it to him. Tom catches it with ease, however, and in one movement slashes the taught line between our two boats. Nick is now free from the line, any line. He is floating in the middle of the ocean.

At this point, a lesser man than Nick would have died. His body is so weak, and the ocean is so strong, that none of us could jump in and save him or we'd risk facing the same fate.

Tom and I shout encouragement helplessly from the deck as Thor quickly tosses him a floatation device on a fresh line. Nick is close now, but even a simple toss is next to impossible when you're rising and falling two stories every 10 seconds.

In what is perhaps the greatest athletic achievement I've ever seen, Nick does what should have been impossible. He swims. He swims to the life preserver and holds it tight. Within seconds Thor has him out of the water and onto the deck of the rescue boat.

A few days later they would hit Cape Verde—the closest land mass with a hospital. Nick would make a full recovery, and Ethan would return to his old life. They were safe.

But we, definitely, were not.

LEADERSHIP LESSON: CONNECT OR REMOVE

For every team, there are only two types of failures: the ones you can control and the ones you can't. Latitude 35 had to endure both.

We had to evacuate two men off of a four-man boat 600 miles into a 3,000-mile race. Tom and I stayed on the boat, but we were not expected to finish. Some experts wondered if we would even survive.

Nick did not choose to leave. Ethan did. The failure of Nick to complete the race was one of biology and ecology. It was not something I could control as a leader. But the failure of Ethan was.

It might be easy to look at Ethan and think, how could he abandon his team like that? But this failure was not Ethan's fault. It was mine.

It's become a cliché now for leaders to take responsibility for other people's mistakes. I don't do this. When someone on my team messes up, they hear about it. Remember, high-performance teams are always personal, and being personal means being honest.

Ethan's leaving was my fault. I knew he wasn't right for the team from the day I recruited him. I saw how he interacted with the other team members, and it wasn't good. But I didn't care. He was a good rower, a great rower, even. And I wanted to win a rowing race, so Ethan stayed on the team.

If I had been an actual leader at that point, I would have given Ethan a ticket home in La Gomera and apologized for wasting his time. I would have seen that Ethan was missing two qualities that every leader should look for when building and leading a high-performance team: malleability and flexibility. And I would have known that I was lacking two elements that every high-performance leader needs: sensitivity and severity.

We've all been on teams with bad eggs, but when that happens, it's important to step back and ask yourself what's really going on. Is your company purposely hiring bad people? Probably not. Nobody ever hires someone they think will do a bad job. But somewhere along the line, all that talent goes to waste.

Teammates on high-performance teams need to be malleable and flexible. This means that when you're building these teams you should spend less time looking at résumés and more time looking at the emotional states of the people you might bring in. Instead of asking interview questions about how many sales they made last year, ask them about a time at work when they did something they didn't want to do and still performed at a very high level. Someone who can answer that question decisively is the sort of person you need on a high-performance team.

But that's what you do if you're building a team from scratch. What if you've inherited a team, or what if you don't have the luxury of being quite so picky? That's when you need to become either sensitive or severe.

Your job as the leader of a high-performance team is to constantly be connecting your team to something greater. But that doesn't always work the way you want it to. Some people just don't get it. In those cases your first step should be to be sensitive—to try to figure out why the person isn't connecting and see what you can do to help them improve things.

But if that fails, you need to be severe. If you cannot connect a person to the same something greater as that of the rest of the team, that person becomes a threat to the goal for everyone. Then your job is to move them to a place where they can hopefully connect with something greater somewhere else. It might be another role, another project, another manager, or another company altogether.

Firing shouldn't be the first thing you consider with a struggling teammate, but it also shouldn't be the last. If you choose to be a leader, you will, at some point, have an Ethan on your team. It's not about firing a bad hire; it's about removing a person who doesn't want the something greater that you're offering.

Back at Sonoma State, Coach Mark let the brutal 5 a.m. workouts decide who was and was not connecting to that something greater. When a member of the team couldn't take it anymore, they stopped coming back. In a similar way, you as a leader need to notice and celebrate who is coming to your 5 a.m. practices.

Leaders need to prioritize and celebrate resilience in their teammates. You can't control the outside forces that will affect you and your team, but you can control how you respond to them. Results are one thing, but watch for the people who achieve good results even when the circumstances change.

Who are the people who raise their hands not just once but consistently, project after project. Who always seem to have too much on their plate? Who never seem all that happy when a project gets completed? Who can never make it to the monthly happy hour?

All these signals will help you find the adaptable people on your team—the people who are connected to your something greater and willing to become whatever it takes to make it happen. On that first Latitude 35 team, Tom was the most connected and adaptable.

On paper, he was the weakest rower, but when the chips were down, he was the one who was ready to endure what came next in order to achieve our shared goal.

The roads that high-performance teams choose to walk are not comfortable. In fact, they're often blatantly painful. That is why you have to be willing to be severe with people like Ethan and why people like Tom are so valuable.

Those are the people who create the teams that can truly do the impossible.

GATHERING POINT:
PRIORITIZE RESILIENCE

>> **It stops with you:** A team member who is creating a toxic work environment is ultimately a failure of the leader.

» **Identify and encourage:** You cannot control the way outside forces act upon you. You can only control how you respond to them. This is known as resilience. Structure your team in a way that reveals and rewards resilience over anything else.

» **Connect or cut:** Everyone wants to be part of something greater than themselves. But if they don't want to be part of your something greater, then you must either convince them to become part of it or move them to a place where they can feel that connection. Anything less is a disservice to that person and an often insurmountable risk to the goal of the high-performance team you are leading.

EAT BREAKFAST

How do people actually work together? Google "management styles," and you'll find out that there are only four real types of leaders. Oops! Actually, it's six. Yikes! Scroll a little farther, and it's seven. No wait, it's ten! And, if you're brave enough to scroll to the bottom of the page, you'll find out there's actually no such thing as a management style; we're all just monkeys fighting over a rapidly shrinking supply of bananas.

But once all of the Myers-Briggs tests and "data-driven" charts are stripped away, all of leadership comes down to that one simple question. How do YOU, as a human being, convince other human beings to execute an action? And it's not the royal "you," either. It's personal.

According to the *Harvard Business Review*, there were more than 23 million managers and frontline business leaders working in the United States in 2016. The writer calls this an excess. And this particular one is costing the US economy more than $3 trillion every single year.

Why? Why do more managers, more structure, and more bureaucracy add up to less productivity, shrinking revenues, and stymied success?

I've spent most of my adult life studying, training, and coaching other leaders. That experience has shown me very clearly why more managers equals less success in America.

The reason is this: most managers don't manage people; they manage the results those people can create.

Of those 23 million managers, I bet that only a small percentage are able to connect with their teams on anything other than business terms. That is why we athletic leaders are sought out by our corporate counterparts so often. Corporate leaders may not know what it is, but they know we are doing something they aren't. Why can our teams summit mountains or hike across entire countries when theirs won't even stay until 5:15 without demanding overtime?

My theory is that the majority of organizational leaders are operating under the misconception that leadership is a right-brain analytical process when, in reality, it's a left-brain emotional experience.

Persuading people, driving the actions you need, won't happen just because you wrote a big number on the whiteboard at the last team meeting. But it will happen once you are able to identify, understand, and leverage the emotions of your team. That's my theory. But, like all good theories, it needs to be proven.

My proof's name is Thomas Magarov.

DECEMBER 2015

The Atlantic Ocean

Days 10 to 54

Rowing a 30-foot boat in the middle of the ocean makes you question the meaning of existence. Doing it at night makes you feel like you don't exist at all. When the sun sets, the few visual anchor points you had vanish along with it. You become a disembodied spirit with only the burn of your muscles and the rasp of your breath keeping you tethered to reality. Without that, you feel as if your essence would calmly drift away from the waves to join the swirling phantasm of stars in the shining canopy above.

Nights on the ocean are usually beautiful beyond words. But ours are not. Two men alone, rowing for 16 hours a day, sleeping every other moment, eating freeze-dried food, and drinking less water than the average housecat—it's all somehow even more brutal than it sounds.

We see some amazing things as we continue toward Antigua, but mostly it is repetitive, boring, and excruciating. To make things worse, we seem to be rowing slower every day.

Tom had far less training than any of the rest of us did before the race. His skills were ready to shine when we had two other men on board, but this new arrangement is not set up to support his skills.

To compensate, I abandon our traditional two-hours-on-two-hours-off schedule in favor of a new strategy: Jason stays on the oars until he's about to pass out.

That isn't to say Tom has it easy. Basically every task on the boat requires two people to be done well. Even something as simple as pumping fresh water has become a nightmare.

The desalinator on our boat is essentially a highly pressurized tube that sucks in water fast enough to create the intense pressure needed to scrub the water of all that pesky sodium. The problem is that this has to be done manually. Basically, you flip a switch on one end of the boat while a teammate listens at the pump. As soon as he hears a click, he tells you to shut the system off immediately.

Going too short could leave toxic salt in your drinking water. Going too long could make the pump explode. Win, win.

When we started the race we had hoped to finish in less than 30 days. But as the sun rises and sets, rises and sets, and rises and sets, our progress seems to grind to a halt. At this point we'll be lucky to reach Antigua in 60 days.

Thirty-two days into the race we are a little over halfway there. Tom and I have been on our own since day 8. It is getting to us.

The connection we felt when he decided to stay with the race feels a million years away. It has been replaced by a silent indifference. We barely speak. We barely look at each other. We just row, sleep, eat, and row.

I begin to contract Nick's penchant for hallucination. On those long rows by myself at night I can swear I hear children crying, dogs barking, and people speaking. In my weaker moments, I sometimes talk back.

By day 40 we realize something has to give or we are going to break.

I'm not saying this is a *Knife in the Water* situation, but I do catch Tom staring at the same blade he used to free Nick just long enough to worry me. I'm kidding. Sort of.

Just like every organization in history, we are going through a crisis. But Tom fixes it with a single question.

One morning while he is preparing his standard pack of freeze-dried monotony, he pauses. Then he turns to me for the first time in ages. "What do you want for breakfast?" he asks.

It is such a simple, human question that it throws me off. After a full minute I finally answer. "Chicken risotto," I croak. My voice sounds foreign and fragile.

"Sounds amazing," Tom responds. "I think I'll have the spaghetti Bolognese. Do you want coffee?"

I laugh. A real, honest-to-goodness laugh. "Hell, yes, I want coffee!" My voice doesn't sound so fragile anymore.

From that day on, no matter what, Tom and I had breakfast together in the morning. We weren't rowing, we weren't pumping water, we weren't scraping the boat for barnacles. We were talking, we were laughing, we were dreaming together again. We were engaging each other's emotions.

After breakfast everything changed. Suddenly, we weren't rowing to finish this stupid race. On that boat, in that ocean, the two of us became what every single team should strive to become: a group of people who are more afraid of letting each other down than anything else in this world.

We both rowed harder and longer than ever before. Not because we were stronger but because we were together. We weren't rowing to prove the headlines about us wrong. We weren't even rowing to shove it in Ethan's face. We were rowing for each other. We were rowing for breakfast.

Every team needs something like this. Your team needs something like this. So what is it? What is the ritual you've created that gives each person on the team the time and focus it takes to engage the others as people, not just as co-workers? It doesn't have to be expensive. It doesn't have to be inventive. It doesn't even have to be particularly interesting.

For us it was two guys eating bad food with good conversation for 20 minutes a day. Yours can be just as simple. Just make sure it's consistent, convenient, and intentional. Emotion matters, so make cultivating it in your team a priority. The results you see won't just speed you toward the finish line. They will be what get you across it.

After 54 days, 8 hours, and 32 minutes, the *American Spirit* entered the port of Antigua and completed the 2015 Talisker Whiskey Atlantic Challenge.

This was a feat that more than one journalist covering the race had already called "impossible"—in fact, one of them even said we were selfish for even trying and all we were doing was risking the lives of the rescue boat that would eventually be dispatched to help us. But we didn't just finish. We did a hell of a lot more.

After the evacuation, we were in third-to-last place. But after our breakfast moment, we were able to finish in eleventh place out of 23.

LEADERSHIP LESSON:
RECOMMIT

Everyone in the world who was following the Talisker that year seemed to think that it was only a matter of time until we dropped out. People set world records all the time, so even though we didn't even win the race, I still believe there's an element to this particular race that goes beyond being the best in the world. That element is, what happened?

What Tom and I put together was leveraging human emotion at its pinnacle. During breakfast, we rediscovered each other as emotional beings, and in doing so we created a small but very high-performance team. This was a team of two, but those two people had become completely interdependent.

Before breakfast we were afraid of the ocean, afraid of our failures, afraid of having to quit the entire race. But after we started our little ritual, our list of fears dropped to one: letting the other guy down.

The former fears were threatening to destroy us, but the latter fear began to fuel us. Every problem was attacked together, every stroke was taken with a little more ferocity, every shift got 100 percent of our effort. There was no way we would fail each other. And by not failing each other, we also avoided failing in the race.

All high-performance teams need diversity. Diversity provides access to different perspectives, and that's exactly what this world needs. But high-performance teams also have to focus on what they have in common in very practical ways.

As a leader, this means re-answering the question *why?* for your team. That's what breakfast was for us. Connecting emotionally like that was a daily reminder of why we were working so damn hard. Becoming a high-performance team means becoming interdependent, and becoming interdependent means giving your team these breakfast-like opportunities to connect.

Most leaders don't like setting their teams up this way. When prominent executives leave a big company, the companies always portray it in the press as if it's no big deal. But if losing a member of your team is no big deal, then you don't have a team at all.

Think about a sports team that wins back-to-back championships. That's incredibly rare, and three in a row is so rare that as soon as a team does it, it is automatically considered to be one of the greatest of all time. But why is it so hard to repeat? It's because it's hard to keep a team together. High-performance teams are so interdependent that if one guy gets traded or twists his ankle, the whole ship comes crashing down.

It's important to note that you can have a team that does a great job of checking in with one another that still misses the mark of high-performance. That's because the emotional component of checking in, not the practical one, makes the difference.

You can't just have a weekly meeting. You need to have a weekly meeting that people look forward to and feel the need for in their hearts. You can't just create gathering points. You need to create the gathering points that your team craves.

For us breakfast was a gathering point that was so rich that it literally changed the way we felt not only about what was happening but also about the way we performed.

The pushback I get on my ideas most often is this: well, that worked for you on the ocean but I'm just a [insert mundane job here]. Leaders want to know this: how do you re-create the emotional desperation of being adrift at sea when you're in a comfortable office with plenty of free snacks? The answer is simple: you need to make things more difficult for your team.

This advice cuts against the grain of what most leaders are trying to do for their teams: cutting down stress and making life easier overall. But let me just say this: if your environment is mundane, it means you are not asking enough of the team you lead.

Gathering points become rich once they are needed, not once they are entered on a calendar. If there's no challenge, who cares about checking in with one another? But when the heat is on, team members need to see one another. They're desperate to. Checking in is the only hope they have of hitting this massive and impossible goal. So if the people on your team aren't feeling the need to recommit with one another at this level, then as their leader you need to turn up the heat.

Properly leveraging human emotion means that a person is more afraid of letting their teammates down than they are of anything else. It raises the amount of sacrifice and suffering a person is willing to go through in order to achieve their goal by harnessing the power of the relational bonds that exist between all humans. That's what breakfast did for us. It didn't make us stronger or faster. But it reminded us that we were human.

Our priority shifted from trying to row a certain number of miles a day to remembering why we were rowing those miles in the first place. Re-answering the question *why?* for both Tom and me every morning became the most important thing in the world. If you're a leader, it should become the most important thing to you for your team as well.

In reality, the process is 99 percent of achieving a goal; the outcome is just that final 1 percent. What you as a leader do and how you respond to your team during the process is what determines whether your team becomes truly high performance.

Simply achieving your goal or outperforming the competition will not be enough to get your team to recommit. You must find ways to explain and celebrate the process more than you explain and celebrate the outcomes you want the process to achieve.

You have to do this with discretion and always from the mind-set of leveraging emotions, not breaking them. But, trust me, humans want to make emotional connections, they want to push past their limits, and good leaders give their people the opportunity to do so.

JANUARY 2016

The Finish Line—English Harbor, Antigua

On the last day of the race, Tom is giddy, almost drunk with excitement. He laughs uncontrollably and nearly bursts into song when we finally see land. He has done what he set out to do. He has represented his adopted country with flying colors. His race is finally over.

I join in as much as I can. I smile and joke and congratulate him for this amazing accomplishment. He has done what he set out to do. But, for me, something is wrong.

Sure, I am happy to be getting off this damn boat. I am happy I'll soon be eating food that didn't come out of a packet. I am very, VERY happy to be reuniting with my wife.

But part of me—the part that sharpened when I saw Thor getting ready to throw that line—is not happy. That part of me realizes something that the rest of me won't admit for several months, that in life there are moments to rest and moments to quit, but there are also moments to push.

I have just rowed across the ocean. It is the hardest thing I've ever done. It has nearly killed me.

But I know I have to do it again.

GATHERING POINT:
HEALTHY FEAR

>> **Emotion is everything:** Properly leveraging human emotion means that a person is more afraid of letting their teammates down than they are of anything else. It raises the amount of sacrifice and suffering a person is willing to go through in order to achieve their goal by harnessing the power of the relational bonds that exist between all humans.

>> **Stay close to your why:** Re-answering the question *why?* becomes a leader's top priority in any team that is trying to sustain high performance. That's because maintaining that level of output for impossible goals is so difficult,

a leader must understand that their team members are going to need to continually recommit themselves to the team.

≫ **Process over results:** The process is 99 percent of achieving a goal; the outcome is that final 1 percent. What you as a leader do and how you respond to your team during the process is what determines whether the team can maintain their level of output. Simply achieving your desired goal or outperforming the competition will not be enough to get your team to recommit. You must find ways to explain and celebrate the process more than you explain and celebrate the outcomes you want the process to achieve.

MULTIPLY THE MULTIPLIERS

ANGUS

Everything about Latitude 35's race was a surprise. No one expected Nick to get sick or Ethan to leave. No one expected Tom and me to stay, and I'm sure that no one expected us to finish. But another boat in our field had a much more predictable experience.

The *Jean Marie* completed its voyage across the Atlantic in 37 days, 9 hours, and 12 minutes—a decisive and expected victory. The winning team, Ocean Reunion, was the best in the race by far. But, as the saying goes, "Good artists borrow; great artists steal." And I had a massive heist in mind.

As competitors, Angus Collins and I were fundamentally different. Even though I had trained under a classic European coach at Vesper, Angus was born with Yorkshire pudding in his veins. He rowed his way through the legendary Essex program with great success and parlayed that momentum straight to the oceans. Plural.

Before captaining Ocean Reunion to its 2015 Talisker victory, Angus already held a world record for crossing the Indian Ocean in a grueling 70 days. After the Talisker he could arguably be called one of the top-five most successful ocean rowers on the planet, if not the best outright.

Since he was the one who built my boat, I would have called Angus Collins after the race anyway. All those other factors may have crossed my mind as well, but someone else had gotten to him first.

Through our chats Angus revealed that the offers had started pouring in even before the *Jean Marie* touched the dock in Antigua. An entrant in the 2016 Talisker had already offered him $30,000 to captain their crew. For a sport that doesn't usually pay anything, that's a fortune.

As our phone conversation began, I congratulated him, but for some reason Angus seemed ruffled.

"There's just one thing that's bothering me," he growled. "I heard you may be entering again as well. It must have been hell for the two of you to row that four-man boat all the way in. I can't shake the feeling that together we could do something pretty special."

I was shocked. I was the one frantically planning ways to sway him away from five figures, and I never thought he would be the one to bring it up first. "I am looking for a new crew," I replied, trying to sound measured. "But listen, man, I could never be the guy who comes between you and that kind of money. You have to take it."

The line was quiet for a while. And then that beautiful baritone said the one thing that could make me respect this world champion more than I already did. "I hear you, mate, but listen. I'm more interested in making history than I am in making money."

I couldn't believe it, but Angus was in.

ALEX

My strategy for the first race was to try to outsmart the ocean, but I quickly realized how foolish that was. You can't win any games with it because it refuses to even play. It's just an unstoppable force of nature. So I decided to recruit a few of my own.

Angus and I together could easily handle the logistics, navigation, and day-to-day operations of the race. We didn't need another Ethan—for a multitude of reasons—we needed power.

Like I said before, ocean rowing boats need an engine. But this time, I wanted two.

The first was relatively easy to acquire. By signing Angus I had given up on my goal of winning the Talisker with a United States crew. But that's the thing about big goals. They're worth only what you're willing to give up to get them. Which, for me, meant checking my pride and saying a hearty "Hail to the Queen!"

Alex Simpson had rowed with Angus to set that Indian Ocean record. He's bigger and stronger than your average rower with a surprisingly posh, cut-glass accent that couldn't be more different from Angus's. Angus himself recommended Alex to me, and when I asked why, he gave me an honest answer: "The kid just shuts up and rows."

Let me pause here and say how important someone like that is to your organization. Talent is obviously important. Commitment is even more so. But when you're weighing the individual strengths of your team, don't be suckered by flash. Find the people who just shut up and row. Their consistency is what will carry your team when all the loud ones, the type A's, and the overthinkers burn out.

Alex jumped at the chance to row with Angus again. The two of them were born to adventure. If they'd been born a few centuries earlier, they probably would have raced Magellan around the world. With them on board, our team was looking crazy strong. But not strong enough. If we were going to do this right, I knew we'd need some good old-fashioned American muscle.

MATT

This was an important day at Vesper. In just a few seconds, Michiel was going to give the signal, and the seat race would begin. If I won this, I'd finally be going to the show. The big time. The top boat.

My boat won the first race—a great start. But as I switched out of that boat and started settling into the other one, the guy in front of me suddenly turned around. "We're actually faster than the boat you just came from," he told me. "The choppy water was keeping us from getting good connection on the front end. Slow down and focus on staying right with me. Don't be late to the water, and we'll surge ahead. Adjust your spacers to allow you to finish a little higher and get out of the water clean."

I didn't respond; I just went to work adjusting my spacers. Not because of what was said but because of who said it. When Matt Brown talks, people listen.

Matt is six foot five, 240 pounds of "Oh, shit, look at that guy!" He was a track star in high school who, similarly to me, pivoted into rowing at college. His first time on the rowing machine at UCLA, he pulled a 6:20 without any technique or training whatsoever. Once the word got out, the Ivies descended on him like he was Scarlett Johansson at Comic-Con.

When the dust settled, the UCLA on Matt's jersey had been replaced with a big blue Y. By the time I finally got in touch with him, we were pushing June. With little time to train, Angus and I knew that whoever took the fourth spot aboard the *American Spirit* would already have to be at their fighting weight. Matt was the perfect candidate.

Matt came into his own at Yale, then made the team at Vesper, where he quickly shot up to the top boat. After Vesper he earned his master's while rowing abroad for Oxford's legendary crew.

While I was rowing the Atlantic, Matt was gearing up for Olympic trials. Unfortunately for him, he didn't make it. Fortunately, I knew exactly how that felt. I knew how it felt to have talent and strength and to have absolutely nothing to do with them. I knew I could sell him on this challenge, but he wasn't so sure.

Matt had just taken a great job at a tech company in San Francisco, and he had a wife and newborn daughter to support. If I wanted him on board, I would have to be a better leader than I was before. I would have to do more than just recruit. I would have to build a community. I would have to establish a generation.

I was always fascinated with the trophy case at Vesper. Not just because it was full of gold medals but because each of those medals represented one group of people at one time who pulled off one unbelievable accomplishment. For the four years I rowed there, we became the new generation of the historic Vesper program. We could feel it, and we took it seriously.

Sundays were our only day off, so Saturdays were sacred times for the team. We wouldn't leave the bar if one of our guys was still inside. Do you have date? Doesn't matter. You'll be politely calling it an early night with her and meeting up with the team. Because this team matters.

The difference between building a team and establishing a

generation is that teams work for a goal, but generations work for one another. This starts with the leader. It's one thing for you to know when to push, when to rest, and when to quit, but it's another to extend that throughout an organization.

As a leader, you are always trying to do something greater. But not everyone's version of that is the same. In order to bring people into your generation, you need to be able to convince them that they're something greater is or should be the same as yours. Doing this doesn't require standing on your desk and delivering a grand, Braveheart-style speech. It happens day by day, one decision at a time. Matt is a perfect example.

After a few weeks of back-and-forth phone calls and deep discussion with his family, Matt was close to joining the team. He had just one final problem that needed solving. Over the phone he told me that his wife was on board, his new job was supportive, he'd have all the time off he needed. But there was just one problem: daycare.

I almost laughed. Despite his superhuman size and strength, Matt is actually extremely emotional. He cries more than any guy I know who can squat 400 pounds.

Matt's biggest concern wasn't the risk of the race. It was being able to afford childcare so his daughter and wife could be supported while he spent eight weeks with me chasing a dream. I cut him off before he could even finish the request. "Matt—we got it," I said. "I'll put it in the budget."

He started to go on about how much it would cost, but I cut him off again. "Whatever you and your family need, the team will take care of it." That was it. Matt was in.

Every person you are leading has this type of emotional lever. Pulling it may have a cost, but it's always worth paying it. Because once it's flipped, that person won't just be working on your team; they'll be joining you in your generation. Matt's lever was his daughter. Because I was willing to support her, he was willing to support me. And her name, fittingly, is Olympia.

LEADERSHIP LESSON:
INVITE THEM IN

There is a difference between the best guys and the right guys. Every member of my new team was more than a strong athlete. They were all leveraged toward the goal of a world-record row on both a personal and a team level. After my experience with Nick, Ethan, and Tom, I knew that emotion mattered more than anything. And I couldn't stop thinking about how far that idea could take us.

When Tom and I started eating breakfast together and re-engaging with each other emotionally, we went from twenty-third to eleventh place and finished a race most people thought would kill us. But what if instead of just Tom and me there was a four-person boat full of people who were similarly leveraged to and for one another? A team like that, I thought, could do anything. But why stop there?

The more I thought about it, the more I realized that my teammates are not the only people who leverage my emotions. My wife, for example does that better than anyone every day of my life. And, I realized, the men I would be rowing with had wives and daughters and significant others, and fathers and mothers and friends and neighbors as well.

Slowly I began to see the lens zoom out on the unending network of emotional connections that exists behind each and every human being. As I took in these constellations of impossibly strong bonds, I decided that our team would no longer be just the four of us. I realized that it never was to begin with.

All the teams we lead are made up of people who represent many other people. The power of leveraging an individual's emotional connection is impressive. The power of leveraging that entire gamut of interdependency is quite frankly unstoppable.

Once you realize that the junior assistant on your team is actually the product of an infinitely complex web of emotional connections, you should jump at the chance to leverage that web for the purposes of your high-performance goal. This is how you do it.

Once a quarter, invite your teammates to bring the people they most care about to a meeting about their jobs. I know, it's crazy; nobody does that. Whenever we talk about work-life balance, we're mostly talking about keeping work out of the home, not bringing the home directly in to work. Uniting as much of your team's emotional network under the banner of your team's goal is unspeakably powerful.

If your junior salesman's wife suddenly sees her husband's office, listens to his boss explain the team's goals, has the chance to meet other members of the team and ask as many questions as she wants, she will leave better prepared to leverage his emotions in your team's favor.

Then the conversations they have at dinner about work won't be so one-sided. Then she can understand better why he's staying late and can provide more empathy or higher-quality feedback. Suddenly, the most powerful emotional lever in his life is leveraging him toward your team's shared goal as well. That lever is a multiplier on that teammate's performance that will unlock unbelievable results. I say so from experience.

I had two years to train for my first Atlantic crossing. The new team would have only nine months. Matt and I trained in the Bay Area while Angus and Alex worked together in England. The days passed in a flurry of protein intake, international phone calls, and list making, until finally, the new Latitude 35 would come together in person at last.

A few weeks before we would head out to the starting line in La Gomera, I flew Angus and Alex out to California to connect with the rest of the team. But, fascinated by this idea of emotional connections, I also brought out the people they were closest to as well.

The time we spent together was unlike anything I've ever experienced. On one memorable night our group was occupying an entire restaurant in my sleepy little Northern California suburb. All around me I saw people laughing, talking, listening, and making new friends over good food. At that moment I truly realized what Michiel meant when he talked about earning your medals in the off season. Looking at the people in that restaurant, I could feel the strength of the emotions being leveraged. And I knew, beyond any shadow of a doubt, that we were going to win.

But, as always, the ocean had other plans.

JANUARY 2017

The Atlantic Ocean

We're screwed. I rub my charred forehead with salt-caked fingers, hoping to shake loose some inspiration, but all that falls is another flurry of dead and peeling skin.

I close my eyes and try to focus, but there's barely enough room for someone my size to sit in the cabin, let alone come up with an idea to get us out of this mess. I let myself stay like that for a while as we rise and fall on the disturbingly gentle waves, each one a reminder that our dream is slowly dying.

Eventually, I have to face the facts: This isn't just a mess, it's a disaster, and we don't need a good idea.

We need a miracle.

GATHERING POINT:
THE TEAM BEHIND YOUR TEAM

» **The right people:** There's a difference between having the best people on your team and having the right people on your team. Talent must be only part of the overall picture when you're building a high-performance team.

» **See the network:** Understanding who has the power to leverage your teammates' emotions, and who they in turn have the power to emotionally leverage, is the key to understanding who your teammates truly are.

» **The actual team:** In business, most people identify the team as the people who are getting paid to accomplish the task. But if a husband, wife, best friend, or neighbor leverages a teammate, then you must see them as being part of the solution as well. If more people are leveraging and being leveraged, both within and outside of your organization, then the amount of suffering and sacrifice your teammates will be willing to endure will increase exponentially. This is the key to creating a truly exceptional team.

EIGHTY-MILE DAYS

In the introduction, I talked about building one incredible team and learning lessons along the way. Angus, Alex, Matt, and I were that team.

Together, we exhibited all the signs of a truly high-performance team. We were completely interdependent. We were all aligned to the same something greater. We all had strong whys for racing, and as the leader I was prepared to answer that question for my team every single day. Most importantly, we were 100 percent leveraged emotionally to and for one another.

All four men who stepped into that boat were products of the emotion-first leadership system I'd been putting together for over a decade. As I said earlier, high-performance teams need to become high-performance before the actual test that will define them as such. In my opinion, we were already a high-performance team before taking a single stroke.

But then we had to face our test.

LATITUDE 35 2.0

My second Atlantic crossing could not have been more different from my first. This was the most capable team I had ever put together, and it was also the most capable team to ever row the Talisker. Early news coverage was calling us a "superteam," and we lived up to the hype.

Having Angus on board was transformational. His experience and skill on the open ocean is unparalleled. Together, we crafted what we considered the perfect route to the finish line.

We accounted for every mile. We considered every possible advantage or disadvantage. We did everything we could to reduce the environmental variable so we could focus on our biggest strength: strength.

A few days into the race, Matt gave me flashbacks of Nick by showing signs of acute seasickness. But by the time we hit the 1,000-mile milestone, he had rallied. I honestly don't know if his symptoms subsided or if he was just too damn strong for them to slow him down. People say that I'm like a machine, but Matt is an animal.

True to his reputation, Alex talked less and rowed more than anyone else on the crew. Because of his inability to grow the thick, lustrous adventure beards that the rest of us were sporting, we teased him regularly about being our resident "baby." He'd laugh sheepishly, but I honestly think the reason his hair follicles were growing so slowly is because every ounce of testosterone in his body was going to fuel our work. Because of him and Matt, the *American Spirit* was moving faster than she ever had before.

Together, we locked comfortably into the two-hours-on-two-hours-off strategy that I had never really put in practice during my first attempt due to all the setbacks we faced. Two hours of sleep may not sound like a lot, but it beats the hell out of 40 minutes. Latitude 35 2.0 was in full force. But we weren't the only boat on the water.

Angus and Ocean Reunion had left a massive power vacuum when they disbanded. I like to think Latitude 35 was able to fill most of it, but every competitor has its opposite number. For this race, the role of rivals would be played by Row4James—a team of four strong, skilled, young Englishmen.

Every morning, Angus and I got on the sat phone for an update from Tom and the rest of our land team. The update always included a weather report, an analysis of our pace, and routing recommendations. But we also made sure to get an update on R4J as well. They were giving us one hell of a race.

As we crossed the halfway point, we were in first place, with a close but respectable lead. We were also on track to break the previous world record. We were progressing exactly as planned.

Which should have been my first clue that things were about to go horribly, horribly wrong.

JANUARY 2017

The Atlantic Ocean

Day 17

With only 1,000 miles to go, things start falling apart. Literally.

If there were a Wikipedia entry for "things that should never, ever be mixed," the number one entry would be "salt, and anything that is not potato chips." Salt destroys things. It's like a thousand tiny locusts that can get inside just about anything to create friction and start chemical reactions that cause decay. If salt had its way, we'd be the ones reduced to dust and trapped in shakers. Salt is a jerk.

Normally, this isn't a problem. Salt might be mean, but it doesn't spread. Unless you physically pour it onto your steak, it can't give you heartburn. But on the ocean salt gets an MVP assist from miles and miles of crashing, spraying, energetic water. The water brings it onto the boat, spreads it around, dries, and leaves the sodium chloride behind to fulfill its dark ambitions. By day two of an ocean row, everything is covered in salt, including you.

The discomfort of being caked in salt 24 hours a day is almost indescribable. Anywhere where salt can get in, it grinds and creates friction. At first you're itchy, then you begin to chafe, and then your skin starts to erupt into open salt sores. To make things worse, the only way to wash yourself off out there is to jump into the ocean. You know, the place where all the salt is.

By the time we hit 2,000 miles, each of us is covered in these sores, which present a very real risk of infection. In addition, each of us has picked up our own unique malady. Angus has a broken finger, Alex has a fractured rib, Matt has torn his shoulder, and I have an infected heel. These are real issues, but our bodies are not my biggest concern at the moment.

The only thing that hates salt more than skin is electronics. By the time we get to 2,000 miles, not only are our bodies starting to flake away before our eyes, but the vital electronics that keep us on course and in touch with the mainland are starting to malfunction.

We realize that we've been pushing things way too hard. If we don't slow down, either the *American Spirit* will break, or we will.

Angus and I do some calculations. We come up with a plan that will allow us to work in more breaks and more time for maintenance without losing our lead. It is a good plan, a great plan even. But it is doomed.

The ocean has turned to glass.

JANUARY 2017

The Atlantic Ocean

Day 29

Most people think that your worst fear when rowing on the ocean is a storm. Sure, when the waves get bigger than your house, it can be a little unsettling. But that also means you're going fast, very fast.

The worst thing that can happen isn't a storm; it's being on the wrong side of one. Even without a sail, wind is everything out on the ocean. When it's blowing, the water's moving, and so are you. But when it stops, you may as well be rowing your way through hair gel.

With 500 miles to go, we have been on the ocean for 28 days. We are 185 miles ahead of R4J and 24 hours ahead of the world record. But then the wind stops, and so do we.

A storm has appeared on the weather report, a storm that has no logical reason to be there. But I shouldn't have been surprised; the only thing the Atlantic is consistent at is inconsistency.

At this point we are already rowing what's called "three up." This means that three people are on the oars at all times while only one rests. This means everyone gets more rowing time and less sleeping time. It's not like Christmas, but we have to be prepared.

The effects of the impending storm will be twofold.

First, while we approach it, we have no wind. The weather is against us, meaning any progress will be difficult. With no wind to help offset the currents, we'll be lucky if we manage to just stay still.

Second, when we do finally hit the storm, we will have wind, lots of wind. But not the wind we want. This wind will come at us from all sides, forcing us to deactivate the autotiller and steer manually. Once again, the odds of making any meaningful progress are basically zero.

This news is devastating. According to the projections, this storm will shrink our lead on R4J to a razor-thin margin. And it effectively wipes out our chances of achieving the world record. That goal has become impossible.

So I find myself crammed into the *American Spirit*'s claustrophobic cabin, rubbing the salt and shredded skin off my forehead, and trying to will a plan into place. But nothing comes.

There is no "solution" to this problem, and problems without solutions are the ones that truly test the mettle of high-performance teams. The only way to achieve the goal we are all leveraged toward achieving is to do something nobody has ever done before. Right there, in the middle of the raging ocean, Latitude 35 will have to do the impossible.

The storm has destroyed our pace. By the time we've fought our way through on manual steering, our speed has gone from 3.0 knots to 0.8 knots. It is worse than we thought it was going to be, and my team needs a plan.

Crunched into that cabin, I push away the maps, turn away from the GPS, and take out my notebook. I close my eyes and let myself start to think.

I'm not sure how long I spend in there. I'm guessing at least a good hour or two. By the time I open the door to face my anxious team, my brain has done its job; the problem has been solved. I have a plan, and it is absolutely insane.

We have 400 miles left to go—400 miles exactly. We have five days left to beat the world record. Even a rower can do math like that. The answer is clear. In order to hit our goal, we will have to row 80 miles every day for the next five days.

The fact that most readers don't gasp at that means that I should probably explain. What I just said does not happen. Some would even say that it cannot happen.

A great day in the Talisker is 70 miles. Any team averaging that would break the world record. It's a fantastic pace that requires an elite crew pulling at 100 percent for 100 percent of the time.

A 75-mile day is extraordinary. Maybe your big engine guys had an extra helping of freeze-dried pierogis that morning. Maybe a friendly whale gave you a little shove. It's cause for celebration. Eighty-mile days are almost unheard of. They require a powerful storm to push the boat at a pace outside of expected human limitations. You might get one in a race this long. We need five, and there are no more storms in sight.

This is it. This is my plan. The only way forward is the way forward. Our goal has been locked inside a vault. The only way in is to tear the door off the hinges. That's not something a person is supposed to be able to do, but there is only one way to find out.

I have reached the greatest test of my career as a leader. This will be the defining moment of my life's work. The way my team reacts will confirm whether or not quitting like a winner, learning how to rest, making bad decisions in a good way, motivating individually, answering the question *why?* and leveraging human emotion works.

I have been trying so hard to become a good leader that I never realized the biggest truth of leadership. You have to make good decisions. You have to put in the time. You have to care. But, ultimately, your success isn't up to you. It never was. It's up to them.

This is the test that will truly measure whether or not we are a high-performance team. The test is not whether we can or cannot row 80-mile days. The test is whether or not my team will even try.

Matt is the first to respond. "Thank God," he says. "I thought you were going to say something like 100 miles a day." He looks around at the others. "You guys don't actually think this is out of reach do you?"

"Not at all, mate," Alex responds. "I'll do whatever you need me to do, skip. I'll row all night if I have to."

Now it is Angus's turn. A silence takes over the boat as we wait to hear his opinion. Three out of four will not cut it. If Angus is out, we all are. "When Jason and I agreed to team up for this year's race," he says at last. "It was with the assumption that we had a better chance at history together than we did apart."

He takes another pause. "I'll be honest when I tell you that I wasn't sure how well we'd work together. But now...we're brothers." I nod my head in agreement. Angus turns back toward Matt and Alex. "And so are we." They nod also.

"We aren't the same guys who went into this. We're different. Jay gave us that." He looks me dead in the eyes. "You gave this to all of us. All we asked for was a chance at history. Well, boys, here it is: five days to row 400 miles. It's not a very good chance, but it's our chance. And I personally wouldn't want to be taking it with any other team."

This moment, hearing these words from my team, is the pinnacle of my athletic career. It is better than any finish line I have ever crossed. This team—a team that I built in the hopes of finally becoming the type of leader I always dreamed I could be—has just shattered the only expectation that really matters: mine. After that moment, I can never be the same.

LEADERSHIP LESSON: BE CHANGED

When you do what we did out there on the water, you are giving yourself wholeheartedly to a goal you believe with all your might is worthy of yourself. When you do that, when you surrender yourself completely to the process, it changes you. It always changes you.

Accomplishing that goal requires you to thoroughly leverage the emotions of your team, but it also means that they will leverage yours as well. When you get to a moment like I did, and you will, and this team that you now genuinely love succeeds in the exact moment you need them to, you will not walk away from that moment the same way you entered it.

Some people aren't interested in that. They don't really want to be changed by their goals or their teams. And, to be honest, there's nothing objectively wrong with that. You can have a perfectly fine career being an individual contributor to a company. Seriously.

You can punch the clock and have a terrific life. But you will not reap the rewards of being on a high-performance team or of leading one. If you want those things, you have to give yourself to something greater than yourself. You have to be vulnerable.

Doing the strong thing means showing a lot of weakness. But the reason I, and others like me, do what we do is because there is an intense reward that comes from identifying an object you think might be too heavy for you to move, setting your shoulder against it, and pushing as hard as you can. Because if you are actually able to move that massive weight, you'll never doubt your own strength in the same way again. Ever.

Self-confidence does not exist in a vacuum. It has to be earned, and the best way to earn it is to attempt something you didn't think you'd be able to do. This is true for teams as well, but at an even larger scale. Big goals can bring self-confidence, but impossible goals require a team.

Achieving those brings you something beyond confidence. It's a form of transcendence that shows you not only how powerful you can be as a single person but how powerful we can all be as people who work together. That's the real goal of high-performance leadership.

It's not just about hitting that sales number or winning that race. It's about you and your teammates discovering together what can happen when emotional human beings connect and commit to a goal. Once you see that, you'll be changed.

You'll never again hear a story like mine and say, "I could never do something like that." You'll say, "I am going to do something even greater."

Every step of the high-performance process in this book is designed to help you move those immovable objects with your team. But, fair warning, once you do that, you won't be the same person you were before. And neither will your teammates.

Together, each of you will have become someone exceptional. Someone powerful. Someone with true, earned confidence. Someone impossible.

JANUARY 2017
The Atlantic Ocean

Days 32 to 35

The first day after we realized our predicament we rowed 79 miles. The next day we did 94 miles. Then 91 miles.

With just 48 hours until the expiration of the chance for a world record, we have only 136 miles to go. The team is driving the *American Spirit*'s jaws around the jugular of the Atlantic Ocean. And, for the first time, the unbeatable ocean suddenly feels mortal. But so are we.

With 48 hours left, we have little left in the tank. We are sleeping for only 40 minutes or less and then rowing for a minimum of two hours. Matt especially has kicked into high gear. He routinely ends his shift only to strap back in for another one. But our efforts are taking a toll.

All of us are hallucinating. At one point Angus taps me on the shoulder to warn about the old lady running around the boat trying to smack us with an oar. I am having visions as well, but mine are a little more serious.

I see people: the people who have mentored me, coached me, and molded me over the years into the exhausted but powerful leader I have become. I see Mark and Michiel, I see my dad, I see Don Wiper and my sponsors. I talk to them, and they talk to me. I can never remember their responses, but I always remember their lessons.

As the sun goes down on January 17, I come off my shift, switching with Angus in a quick 15-second interchange that he and I have performed more than 200 times now.

I heave myself into the cabin to figure out where we stand. I know we have been weak that day. There is no way we've been keeping up with our 90-mile pace of the past few days. I'll be surprised if we've hit even 70 miles. For a moment I feel that we have been defeated, but then I check the map. I start crying.

Eighty-eight miles. We have gone 88 miles on our "weakest" day so far. That means we have to cover only 48 miles in the final 24 hours. We are ahead of Row4James. We are hours ahead of the world record. We are going to do the impossible.

In the late afternoon of January 18, 2017, Latitude 35 crossed the coordinates of 17 degrees north, 61 degrees west, which marked the official finish line of the Talisker Whisky Atlantic Challenge. It took us 35 days, 14 hours, and 3 minutes to cross it, breaking a 13-year-old world record by a shockingly close 11 hours. My team achieved our something greater.

Together, Latitude 35 has made history.

Now it's your turn.

GATHERING POINT: BECOME IMPOSSIBLE

» **Plan to change:** If you choose to give all of yourself to a certain endeavor, you should expect to be changed by it forever. This is the consequence of being part of a high-performance team. As a leader, this is ultimately the trade-off you must be comfortable with for yourself, and for others.

» **Mercenaries:** Those who say no to being part of a high-performance team can still be great individual contributors to a larger organization. There is nothing wrong with that, and every organization needs those people as well. But they are not the people who make up high-performance teams.

>> **The high-performance leader:** As a leader, you help others achieve their goals by building trust and acting authentically and selflessly toward them. When the moment comes that separates good teams from high-performance teams, you will have to look them in the eye and ask for nothing less than everything they have. If you practice what you've learned in this book, they will look straight back at you, and give it.

EPILOGUE:
The Process of Processing

MAY 2018

The Namib Desert, Southwestern Africa

I'm alone. Even with my eyes closed, the sun is still bright enough to make me see spots. I manage one more step before my legs betray me. As I crumple to the ground, the burning sand sears the throbbing blisters on my palms.

As my breathing steadies, I take stock of the situation. The ocean was difficult, but this—this is just brutal. I struggle into a sitting position and fight the urge to take a sip from my hollow canteen. I have no idea where the next water source will be.

I can feel the flaming tongues of panic starting to lick at the back of my mind. I have to make a decision, fast. But my body feels broken, and my mind is blank.

Fortunately, I came prepared. I rummage through my dusty pack until my fingers brush against familiar edges. It's not a sat phone or a Bear Grylls–approved survival knife. It's a small black Moleskine notebook.

LEADERSHIP LESSON:
WRITE AND REFLECT

Reflection and contemplation aren't just for lazy Sunday afternoons. They are the means by which incredible solutions are discovered for impossible problems. Your mind is your best resource. It's a catalyst for miracles.

I've mentioned before that I have a few fundamental skills. One is my ability to suffer longer, harder, and more efficiently than the average person. Another is my ability to identify the best goals for me and my teams in almost any situation. But my final gift is one you may not expect from a professional jock.

I daydream. A lot. And you should too.

As you can probably tell, I'm fascinated with human performance. The things we can do, the limits we can reach, are astounding. And that's not limited to the realm of the physical.

Our brains are powerful, more powerful than any wave, storm, or other mishap could ever be. In any situation, no matter how intense, as long as there is some physically possible solution to be found, the six inches of gray matter between your ears will be able to find it. Solving problems is what all of our brains were built to do.

You don't have to be an Ivy League professor or a surgeon to use this ability. The issue with most people is not that their brain is too weak to get the job done; it's that they never even give it a chance to try. When things start going off the rails, our first course of action is usually to act. It's only natural; it's a primal reflex. But we've come a long way from *Homo erectus*, and your mind is up for more of a challenge.

Accessing the problem-solving power of your mind is not about pushing; it's about stopping. Mental processes are at their most effective during times of stillness, but we've stopped giving ourselves that opportunity.

From sunup to sundown we're all shoving an unending cavalcade of information into our minds. The meeting is at six. Traffic is horrible today. I hate my interns this summer. This podcast is amazing. I love *Game of Thrones*. I should work on that expense report. I wonder if I have time to call Mom before bed. Snore.

Because we keep forcing our minds to process, we never give them space to think, and by doing so, we take away their ability to solve. It's a simple problem to fix. Turn off the tap. Take away all that input, and I think you'll be amazed by your new outputs.

Drive to work with the radio off. Sit in your hammock without a Kindle. Hold your spouse without speaking, listening to music, or watching TV. Take a page out of my book from the Atlantic, and just...be.

Once you start, your mind will go to work. Don't fight it. This isn't about meditation; the goal isn't to stop thinking. It's to start thinking properly.

The more time you give yourself in this form, the better you will get at thinking. Your brain will start to prioritize quicker, analyze faster, and serve up better solutions. This is the greatest superpower of the human race. Stop wasting it.

Everything you've read in this book has come from this exact process. I daydream constantly. I miss almost every TV show that anyone cares about, but I don't mind. I may not know who Jon Snow's real father is, but my notebook is full of ideas, it's full of visions, it's full of solutions. But my story isn't the only one worth telling.

If you took the time to engage with this process, you would start seeing the lessons in your own life. You could write a book of your own. I'm not afraid of a little competition.

Give yourself time. Turn off the tap. Use your mind as it was meant to be used. And write stuff down as often as you can. You never know who might end up reading it.

ONWARD

I snap the Moleskine shut and take a deep, steadying breath. The endless ocean of sand stretches around me in all directions. I'm no closer to my goal than I was before I fell, but now my mind has done its job.

I have an idea. I have a solution. I have a plan.

I stand shakily to my feet and point myself west. It's time to put one foot in front of the other again. It's time to go to work.

ACKNOWLEDGMENTS

This book is the product of a high-performance team.

It would not have been possible without the time, talents, and emotional leverage provided to me by dozens of amazing partners. I am forever grateful for their contributions.

Thank you to my beautiful wife, Amelia. Everything I have and all that I am is because of you. I look forward to a lifetime of adventures together.

Thank you to the entire team at Berrett-Koehler for helping me find the heart of this book and get it to the finish line. Thanks to Jeevan Sivasubramaniam for reaching out and bringing me into the BK family in the first place. And thanks to Sarah Modlin for her passionate voice and true commitment to the quality of this project. Berrett-Koehler has been an amazing partner that never let me settle for anything less than the best this book could possibly be. It is better because of you.

Thank you to Chris Coke and Carlisle for giving me stories to tell in the first place, and Booking.com for giving me a platform to share those stories with the world. Without you, the impossible never would have happened. I look forward to pushing the boundaries together in the future.

Personal thanks to Jeff and Shelby Fautt for their unwavering belief in what I do, both on the water and in the classroom. To Ian Hogg, who showed me by example that family is the foundation of success. To Garry Spence, who is one of the greatest examples of an authentic leader I have ever met. And to Mike Durbin, for refusing to let a single spliced comma, broken tense, or split infinitive go uncorrected.

Finally, thank you to my teams past, present, and future. Thank you for giving me more than I earn and better than I deserve. Our road is filled with impossible challenges. But I'm loving every minute of it.

Adventure is everywhere. Go live yours.

INDEX

ABOUT THE AUTHOR

Jason Caldwell is a professional adventurer, author, and business coach. He is the founder and president of Latitude 35—a professional development and leadership-training organization headquartered in Northern California.

Jason set a world record in 2017 for rowing across the Atlantic Ocean in 35 days, 14 hours, and 3 minutes. Latitude 35 teams challenge the limits of what's possible around the world and currently hold more a dozen world records set across five continents.

Jason teaches at top-tier institutions including Columbia Business School, Wharton School at the University of Pennsylvania, and the Haas School of Business at the University of California, Berkeley. He also travels the world conducting executive leadership programs for Fortune 500 companies, including Nike, Booking.com, and Santander Bank.

Jason currently resides in Danville, California, with his wife, Amelia, and his son, Tristan.

Berrett-Koehler
Publishers

Berrett-Koehler is an independent publisher dedicated to an ambitious mission: *Connecting people and ideas to create a world that works for all.*

Our publications span many formats, including print, digital, audio, and video. We also offer online resources, training, and gatherings. And we will continue expanding our products and services to advance our mission.

We believe that the solutions to the world's problems will come from all of us, working at all levels: in our society, in our organizations, and in our own lives. Our publications and resources offer pathways to creating a more just, equitable, and sustainable society. They help people make their organizations more humane, democratic, diverse, and effective (and we don't think there's any contradiction there). And they guide people in creating positive change in their own lives and aligning their personal practices with their aspirations for a better world.

And we strive to practice what we preach through what we call "The BK Way." At the core of this approach is *stewardship,* a deep sense of responsibility to administer the company for the benefit of all of our stakeholder groups, including authors, customers, employees, investors, service providers, sales partners, and the communities and environment around us. Everything we do is built around stewardship and our other core values of *quality, partnership, inclusion,* and *sustainability.*

This is why Berrett-Koehler is the first book publishing company to be both a B Corporation (a rigorous certification) and a benefit corporation (a for-profit legal status), which together require us to adhere to the highest standards for corporate, social, and environmental performance. And it is why we have instituted many pioneering practices (which you can learn about at www.bkconnection.com), including the Berrett-Koehler Constitution, the Bill of Rights and Responsibilities for BK Authors, and our unique Author Days.

We are grateful to our readers, authors, and other friends who are supporting our mission. We ask you to share with us examples of how BK publications and resources are making a difference in your lives, organizations, and communities at www.bkconnection.com/impact.

Dear reader,

Thank you for picking up this book and welcome to the worldwide BK community! You're joining a special group of people who have come together to create positive change in their lives, organizations, and communities.

What's BK all about?

Our mission is to connect people and ideas to create a world that works for all.

Why? Our communities, organizations, and lives get bogged down by old paradigms of self-interest, exclusion, hierarchy, and privilege. But we believe that can change. That's why we seek the leading experts on these challenges—and share their actionable ideas with you.

A welcome gift

To help you get started, we'd like to offer you a **free copy** of one of our bestselling ebooks:

www.bkconnection.com/welcome

When you claim your **free ebook**, you'll also be subscribed to our blog.

Our freshest insights

Access the best new tools and ideas for leaders at all levels on our blog at ideas.bkconnection.com.

Sincerely,

Your friends at Berrett-Koehler